Praise for *To Garden with God*

"When first created, humans inhabited and communed with God in a garden. We know why, and how all that changed, but what didn't change was our dependence on gardens, or our awe and love of them. Humans and gardens are inseparable. And as we tend our gardens, and consider Christine Sine's profound biblical insights about gardens and gardening, we can once again commune deeply with God—in gardens!"

> **Dr. Chris Elisara,** Founder and Executive Director Creation Care Study Program

"In To Garden with God, Christine Sine shares a profoundly spiritual explanation for the sense of peace we experience when we step into a garden. Blending Scripture with story, this journal—inspirational, contemplative, deeply personal and supremely practical—offers readers a means for transforming pastime into prayer and work into worship. This book is a must-read for seasoned and fledgeling gardeners, and anyone else who yearns to learn how to grow closer to God."

> **Anna M. Clark,** author of *Green, American Style*

To Garden With God

*See how the flowers of the field grow.
They do not labor or spin.
Yet I tell you that not even Solomon in all his splendor
was dressed like one of these.
(Matthew 6:28-29)*

by Christine Sine

Mustard Seed Associates

A resource of Mustard Seed Associates
www.msainfo.org

Join us in creating the future one mustard seed at a time.

Believing God is changing the world through mustard seeds—the seemingly insignificant—MSA seeks to unleash the creative potential of ordinary people to make a difference in their communities and a world of urgent need.

2009 © Christine Sine
Photos by Christine Sine, Tom Balke, Andy Wade, Tara Malouf, and Eliacin Rosario-Cruz. Used with permission.
Published in e-book format May 2009. Revised and republished August 2010.
This work may not distributed in any form electronic or printed or without written permission of the publisher.

Cover photo © Christine Sine, 2008

Scripture taken from the HOLY BIBLE, NEW INTERNATIONAL VERSION®. Copyright © 1973, 1978, 1984 Biblica. Used by permission of Zondervan. All rights reserved.

Scripture marked TNIV taken from the HOLY BIBLE, TODAY'S NEW INTERNATIONAL VERSION®. Copyright © 2001, 2005 by Biblica®. Used by permission of Biblica®. All rights reserved worldwide.
"TNIV" and "Today's New International Version" are trademarks registered in the United States Patent and Trademark Office by Biblica®. Use of either trademark requires the permission of Biblica.

Some scripture taken from The Message. Copyright © 1993, 1994, 1995, 1996, 2000, 2001, 2002. Used by permission of NavPress Publishing Group.

Scripture quotations marked (CEV) are from the Contemporary English Version Copyright © 1991, 1992, 1995 by American Bible Society, Used by permission.

Scripture quotations marked NLT are taken from the Holy Bible, New Living Translation, copyright 1996, 2004. Used by permission of Tyndale House Publishers, Inc., Wheaton, Illinois 60189. All rights reserved.

To all backyard gardeners who have discovered the joy of connecting more intimately to God as they work in the midst of God's creation.

Table of Contents

Introduction 9

To Garden With God 17
    Getting Our Hands Dirty 19
    She Thought He Was the Gardener 22
    God Is Moving: Creating a Faith-Based Community Garden 25
    Organic Gardening 101 30
    Garden Strategies 34
    Gardening as Spiritual Practice 38
    Garbage Into Gold 41

Winter: A Season for Quiet and Retreat 45
    Winter Pruning 47
    Waiting for the Light 50
    Dreaming Big 52

Spring: A Season of New Life 57
    Garden Resurrections 59
    Birds, Spiders, and Prophets 62
    Tomato Theology 66

Summer: A Season for Growth 73
    Growing God's Way 75
    Companion Planting 78
    Watering: Baptizing the Garden 81
    Summer Feasting Recipes 85

Autumn: A Season of Abundance   91

   Pumpkins Don't Leave Holes   93
   Harvest of Plenty   97
   Walk Through the Garden Soup   100
   Recipes for Giving Thanks   104

Praying in the Garden   111

   Garden Blessings   113
   Morning and Evening Prayers for Gardeners   117

Garden Resources   127

   Helpful Books, Catalogs, and Websites   129
   Planting and Harvest Guide and Harvest Log   133

Introduction

The world is charged with the grandeur of God.
It will flame out, like shining from shook foil;
It gathers to a greatness like the ooze of oil.[1]

I have always been a lover of creation, even though as a child I was a very reluctant gardener. My mother is amazed at how keen I have become on gardening because back then I was totally unwilling to go out and pull weeds for her. I think it was really only when I moved to Seattle that I started to become fascinated with the view outside. It is only in the last few years that the garden has become one of my driving passions. So how did this happen?

When my husband Tom and I got married, he had a few tomato plants growing in the side garden and a few scraggly ornamental shrubs in the front. For the first couple of years, I was constantly frustrated because I really wanted to replicate the garden I would have grown in Sydney, Australia. Of course the bougainvillea, hibiscus, and other tropical plants I tried just did not survive the winter

---

1. Gerard Manley Hopkins, *God's Grandeur*, Catherine Phillips, ed. (Oxford, UK: Oxford University Press, 1986), 128.

freeze. So I started reading seed catalogues and that was my undoing. The exotic photos of flowers and vegetables were a temptation I could not ignore. And as the plants started to grow, I discovered that there is nothing quite as delicious as fresh-picked greens in a garden salad. And eating sweet cherry tomatoes straight from the vine is a truly spiritual experience.

My interest in the spiritual significance of gardens grew as I read about early monastic communities that attempted to re-create paradise by planting walled gardens that resembled their idea of Eden. These enclosed spaces were rich with biblical imagery and often centered around an apple tree, representing both the Tree of Life in Genesis and the Cross of Christ.

During the Middle Ages, many plants were renamed with biblical significance. My favorite is the passion flower, native to South America, which was adopted by Spanish missionaries in the fifteenth and sixteenth centuries as a teaching tool. Every part of the flower's bloom became a symbol of a different aspect of Christ's crucifixion. The vine's supporting tendrils represented the whips used to scourge Christ, and the flower's radial filaments, the crown of thorns. The stigmata and anthers represented the nails and wounds. Even the blue and white colors of most passion flowers were symbolic of heaven and purity.

Genesis tells us that God created Adam and Eve and placed them in a garden "to work it and take care of it."[2] Even more intriguingly, we learn that God walked in the Garden of Eden with them. This doesn't surprise me because I always feel that God still walks in the garden with me today. No, don't worry, I am not about to become an animist, but I must confess that most of the best spiritual lessons I learn these days come from the garden rather than from books—and from someone that loves reading as much as I do, that is quite a confession.

During the fourth and fifth centuries, Celtic Christians believed that nature was translucent and that the glory of God shined through it. They have been described as "God-intoxicated people," and as I breathe in the heady aroma of

---

2. Genesis 2:15.

lilacs, I am not surprised. I suspect that these two observations are connected. The more I have looked for God in my garden, the more I have become invigorated by the gospel story and the wonder of God's plan for redemption. As Nancy Ortberg expresses it in her book *Looking For God*, "Nature holds more beauty than our eyes can bear."[3]

I think that one of the reasons people are moving away from Christianity at time-warp speed is that we have divorced our faith from the rhythms and practices of the natural world. Most of our world's population now lives in cities where so much life is totally divorced from God's creation and the rhythms of planting, growing, harvesting, and resting inherent in the garden year. We lose confidence in the story of God because we no longer enter into the constant reminders of death and resurrection that occur in the created.

Yet the gospel still comes to us in the midst of the created world, which was made through Jesus Christ and is being re-created through him. As God's people, we are responsible to love the world with the same love that God has expressed through creation. As a consequence, we must accept God's call to be godly stewards of all that has already been created.

Unfortunately our religious experience is often totally disconnected from God's world. We confine our worship to a small stuffy church building and restrict our devotion to reading words about God without connecting to the glory of God all around us. We can try to re-create an experience of heaven in our churches with bells and smells and rich ornamentation, but that doesn't come close to the wonder of God experienced in the fragrance of flowers, the melody of birdsong, and the beauty of plants and animals.

There is no place quite like the garden for connecting to the story of God. So many of Jesus' parables and the events of his life, death, and resurrection take on new meaning in the garden. I read about the death and resurrection of Christ in

---

3. Nancy Ortberg, *Looking For God: A Unexpected Journey Through Tattoos, Tofu and Pronouns* (Carol Stream, Ill.: Tyndale House, 2008), 16.

the Bible, but I experience it every time I plant a dead seed, bury it in its earthy grave, and watch it burst into life. I read about the faithfulness of God to Israel in the wilderness, but I experience it every time I watch the rainfall nourish the seeds I have planted. I read about the miracle of the fish and loaves, but I experience a miracle every time I am overwhelmed by the generosity of God's harvest.

It seems that there is no better time than this to reconnect our lives to the story of God revealed through the garden. Tough economic times have sent people everywhere scurrying for garden books and packets of seed. Backyard gardening has become an important response of individuals and churches. Even the White House has planted an organic garden to supplement the presidential salads.

Still, few of us seem able to make the direct connections to our faith that there should be. Even much of the theological writing about creation care focuses more on the importance of preserving wilderness areas and overcoming the devastation of pollution than on the joy of gardening. Perhaps part of the reason that God created human beings to tend the garden is because God knew that it would be in the midst of the garden that we would connect most intimately to the character and ways of God.

This journal is a result of fifteen years of reflections and activities as a backyard gardener. I am not an expert gardener, and my garden certainly never looks ordered and pristine like those you see in garden magazines. It is always full of weeds and messiness that would make a Master Gardener cringe. Neither am I a theologian. I always describe myself as a contemplative activist. I have learned my theology through plunging into situations that force me to ask questions about where God is and what God is saying. I suspect that makes me more like the average gardener and the average follower of Christ.

Gardening has taught me to look for God in all my daily activities and encounters. As I watch the days and seasons follow their expected patterns, I am reminded of the faithfulness of a God who comes to us in all seasons and events of our lives. I am also reminded that our God, who poured out his great love in

INTRODUCTION

the complexity, beauty, and diversity of creation, still cares for us and will never abandon what he has made.

Every season of the year teaches new lessons about God that connect to the gospel story. In fact, particularly for those who live in the Southern Hemisphere where the events of the Christian calendar are out of sync with the seasons of the year, I would highly recommend reinventing a liturgical rhythm that flows more with the natural world.

Many of the reflections in this book began as posts on my blog.[4] As people interacted with my thoughts and shared their own garden experiences, I realized that many people first connect to God in the garden. For many of us this continues to be the best place to pray and interact with our Creator and Redeemer.

In this book, we will explore the rhythms of life, death, and resurrection revealed through the garden seasons. At the same time we will discuss the practical aspects of gardening that relate to each season.

Some of the lessons the garden teaches us about God cannot be confined to seasons, so we will begin our journey with thoughts about gardening with God the Master Gardener. Much of our garden time in every season is spent kneeling in the dirt and pulling weeds. Sometimes we just wander through to enjoy the splashes of brilliant color and admire the rapidly growing fruit.

Our journey through the seasons begins in winter, the time when most of the natural world is drawing deep into itself and preparing to rest. The trees retract their sap and drop their leaves. Animals retreat to their lairs to hibernate, and birds flee the cold weather with their flocks. This is the time when we too are meant to slow down and reflect on our lives and our spiritual state. In the Northern Hemisphere, it coincides with the seasons of Advent and Christmas. It is a time for looking inward, for new beginnings and new depths of understanding.

Spring is a time to dig the ground, plant, and fertilize. Bulbs and trees burst into bloom with exultant enthusiasm for a new year. This is the season of great-

---

4. http://godspace.wordpress.com

est activity in the garden when we nurture the newly planted seeds into life and tend the trees that we expect will later provide a rich harvest of fruit. In the Northern Hemisphere, it coincides with Easter, the celebration of Christ's death and resurrection. This is the season when we plant new seeds of faith and cultivate all that will one day blossom and bear fruit in our lives and in God's world.

Summer is the season of abundant growth and productivity. This is when we begin to reap the harvest of our long hours of spring toil. In our spiritual lives, there are also seasons when everything seems to flourish and produce fruit in abundance without much effort on our part. It is a time for both work and fulfillment. In the church calendar, this season begins with Pentecost and the in-filling of the Holy Spirit whose enduring presence enables God's life of love, compassion, and abundance to flourish in and through us. In the church calendar, Pentecost ushers in the second half of the year, what is sometimes called Kingdomtide, the season during which we are meant to live out the life of God's kingdom. Unfortunately we tend to think that this season is forever and when autumn comes, we keep wanting to force feed our lives so that they will continue producing fruit.

Autumn is also a season of great activity as the year culminates in the lavish harvests and the feasting that often accompanies them. In this season we are canning, drying, and preserving the harvest for the days of scarcity that lie ahead. In our lives we need to recognize these seasons when our physical work of gathering in the harvest of our efforts is tempered with the prayer and preparation needed to sustain us throughout the cold seasons of life that assail all of us at times.

Each section of this journal contains spiritual reflections, litanies, and prayers that relate to the season as well as practical suggestions on gardening and an occasional recipe. This is not an authoritative guide to organic gardening, however. That I will leave to the experts. I hope, however, that it will help many who are dabbling in gardening for the first time recognize that we don't need to be experts to enjoy and find satisfaction in the garden.

INTRODUCTION

At the end of the book, there are guides for planting and harvesting that relate to Seattle and the Pacific Northwest, where I live, though they may be useful for other parts of the Northern Hemisphere as well. There is also a resource section that can connect you to some of the best resources I have discovered both on the web and in print.

My prayer is that this journal will not just improve your abilities as a gardener, but that it will also enable you to experience the gospel story in a new and compelling way. To start us off, here is a beautiful Ute Native American prayer that calls us to take notice of the earth and the lessons it can teach us about the God who created it:

Earth, Teach Me to Remember

Earth, teach me stillness, as the grasses are stilled with light.
Earth, teach me suffering, as old stones suffer with memory.
Earth, teach me humility, as blossoms are humble with beginning.
Earth, teach me caring, as the mother who secures her young.
Earth, teach me courage, as the tree which stands alone.
Earth, teach me limitation, as the ant which crawls on the ground.
Earth, teach me freedom, as the eagle which soars in the sky.
Earth, teach me resignation, as the leaves which die in the fall.
Earth, teach me regeneration, as the seed which rises in the spring.
Earth, teach me to forget myself, as melted snow forgets its life.
Earth, teach me to remember kindness, as dry fields weep in the rain.

---

5. Ute American prayer, author unknown.

To Garden With God

Getting Our Hands Dirty

Then the Lord God planted a garden in Eden, in the east and there he placed the man he has made. The Lord God made all sorts of trees grow up from the ground—trees that were beautiful and that produced delicious fruit.[5]

Have you ever thought about the fact that one of God's first acts after creating the world was to plant a garden? I had not really thought about this myself until I received an email recently from Gretchen Tate, a friend from my days with Mercy Ships who works with peasant farmers in developing countries, teaching them sustainable gardening skills. She had just taken a class that looked at the Hebrew roots of biblical words. "I have always been interested in the verse in Genesis that says God *planted* a garden," she told me. "As I broke that passage down into its Hebrew roots, it could be said that the Eternal One surrounded himself with mud. God actually physically *planted* the garden."

How amazing to think that the eternal, omnipotent God who created the universe actually got down in the dirt, got covered in mud, and planted a garden. Of course much of the imagery in Genesis is not meant to be taken literally

---

6. Genesis 2:8-9, NLT

as though God were a human being, but even so, this suggests to me that God was intimately involved and delighted in the planting of the garden. God, in this sense, was like you and me and every other backyard gardener or small farmer. God loves gardening and doesn't mind getting his hands dirty to enjoy it.

There is another verse too that speaks to me of God's love for gardening: "Then the man and this wife heard the sound of the Lord God as he was walking in the garden in the cool of the day."[7] Any avid gardener loves to walk in the garden on a cool summer's evening enjoying the fragrant perfume of nicotinia and the melody of birds. I can just imagine God sharing his delight with Adam and Eve who were created to tend and care for this garden. Can't you see them all walking together, sharing stories, Adam asking advice about how to cultivate and prune the trees, Eve asking for recipes on how best to prepare the luscious fruit? Okay, a little wild imagining there, but you get the picture. Gretchen shared that this idea of God as a gardener has been a wonderful message for the peasant farmers whose lives have been so devalued by societies everywhere. "The eternal God chooses to plant the garden and enter into the work of a farmer, giving life and value to the land and soil and those who partner with him in that. I love that picture," she said.

Unfortunately this picture of God as garden enthusiast is often overlooked as a revelation of the character of God, because of its connection to the story of Adam and Eve being expelled from the garden. We gloss over the activity of God in our grief at the loss of paradise not just for Adam and Eve but for all humanity. But our God is a God who is not afraid to get his hands dirty—not just in the garden, but by entering into every aspect of human life as well.

There are other interesting aspects of the way God created us that suggest we are all meant to be diggers of dirt. British researchers, who are probably all garden enthusiasts themselves, have discovered what many gardeners recognize intuitively: exposure to dirt boosts our happiness. Evidently, lung cancer patients

---

7. Genesis 3:8, NLT

treated with "friendly" bacteria normally found in the soil have anecdotally reported improvements in their quality of life.[8] It doesn't surprise me. There is a growing amount of research that suggests time outside is beneficial in a number of illnesses and complaints. Attention Deficit Hyperactivity Disorder (ADHD) is often dramatically improved if a child spends regular time outside. A recent article in *Organic Gardening* magazine suggested that access to green spaces helps people, especially poor people, live longer and healthier lives. Evidently, access to natural vegetation parks, forests, and rivers cut the otherwise substantial health gap between rich and poor by half.[9]

Other interactions with God's creation are also beneficial. Dog owners don't really need clinical researchers to tell them that their animals make them live longer and healthier lives,[10] and surprisingly, people who are constantly exposed to the pollens of rural living actually have less allergies than those who live in the city.[11]

If this doesn't convince us that God intends all of us to interact with creation, then nothing will. You may not love gardening as I do, but I do believe it is essential for all of us to interact in some meaningful way with creation. And that can take many forms, whether by owning a pet (even a gold fish can be beneficial) or just going for a long walk in the nearest park on a regular basis. It doesn't matter, but some part of the rhythm of all our lives should get us outside for more than a minute or two each day.

---

8. "Dirt Exposure Boosts Happiness," *BBC News* (April 1, 2007), accessed April 22, 2009, at http://news.bbc.co.uk/2/hi/health/6509781.stm.

9. Abigail Poulette, ed., "Tree Huggers are Healthier," *Organic Gardening* (April 2009), 52.

10. Marty Becker DVM, "The Amazing Power of Pets to Heal," accessed April 22, 2009, at http://nursing.msu.edu/habi/Becker.pdf.

11. Carla Helfferich, "Heyday of Hay Fever," Article #995 at the Alaska Science Forum (September 12, 1990), accessed April 22, 2009, at http://www.gi.alaska.edu/ScienceForum/ASF9/995.html.

She Thought He Was the Gardener

Mary Magdalene was standing outside the tomb. . . . She turned to leave and saw someone standing there. It was Jesus, but she didn't recognize him. "Dear woman, why are you crying?" Jesus asked her. "Who are you looking for?" She thought he was the gardener. "Sir," she said, "if you have taken him away, tell me where you have put him and I will go and get him." "Mary!" Jesus said. She turned to him and cried out, "Raboni!" which is Hebrew for Teacher. (John 15:14 - 16)

Why did it matter that Mary Magdalene thought Jesus was the gardener? This is a question that had never occurred to me until I too became interested in gardening. In the midst of the amazing events of the resurrection it seems like a trivial aside that distracts us just when we are holding our breath with anticipation and excitement. Yet nothing in the gospels is there by accident.

Unlike Matthew, Mark and Luke which are called synoptic Gospels because the present the life of Christ with similar content, order and synopsis, the book of John concentrates on themes. One important theme is that Christ will redeem all of creation through re-creation. The gospel of John begins with the words "In the beginning..." which immediately takes us back to the book of Genesis which opens with the same words. "John then lays out a series of events in the life of Christ that mirror the Seven Days of Creation."[12]

---

12. Greg Witherow: *The Gospel of John, Creation and Liturgy*, accessed August 29, 2010 http://www.holytrinityparish.net/Links/The_Gospel_of_John2.pdf

TO GARDEN WITH GOD 23

In Genesis we have already been introduced to God the master gardener. Now we are being introduced to Jesus the gardener of the new creation. In the beginning of the old creation God planted a garden—the garden of Eden. In the new creation, begun through the death and resurrection of Christ, we meet Jesus planting a new garden. The hope and promise of these words which we so often skim over without even thinking about them, is incredible. As we read in 2 Corinthians 5:17, "Therefore if anyone is in Christ he is a new creation, the old has passed away, behold, the new has come."

This new creation is not just a place in which humankind finds wholeness and redemption. This is the new garden and the new gardener that all of God's creation has awaited in eager anticipation and longing. Listen to the beautiful way in which apostle Paul as he talks about this:

> That's why I don't think there's any comparison between the present hard times and the coming good times. The created world itself can hardly wait for what's coming next. Everything in creation is being more or less held back. God reins it in until both creation and all the creatures are ready and can be released at the same moment into the glorious times ahead. Meanwhile, the joyful anticipation deepens.
>
> All around us we observe a pregnant creation. The difficult times of pain throughout the world are simply birth pangs. But it's not only around us; it's within us. The Spirit of God is arousing us within. We're also feeling the birth pangs. These sterile and barren bodies of ours are yearning for full deliverance. That is why waiting does not diminish us, any more than waiting diminishes a pregnant mother. We are enlarged in the waiting. We, of course, don't see what is enlarging us. But the longer we wait, the larger we become, and the more joyful our expectancy.[13]

The book of Revelation also uses garden imagery when it describes the new heaven and the new earth. God's new city is a garden city in which the river of

---

13. Romans 8:18-25, Message

life flows down from the throne of God to bring healing and wholeness to all the nations and to all creation:

> Then the angel showed me a river with the water of life, clear as crystal, flowing from the throne of God and of the Lamb. It flowed down the center of the main street. On each side of the river grew a tree of life, bearing twelve crops of fruit with a fresh crop each month. The leaves were used for medicine to heal the nations.[14]

The gospel stories come alive in the garden, not just because we understand more fully the agricultural parables that Jesus used but also because the garden is a place in which we can truly anticipate God's promise for the future. In the garden, as we watch the plants grow and bring forth fruit in their season it is not hard to believe that one day all creation will indeed be made renewed, restored and made whole to become all that God intends it to be.

---

14. Revelation 22:1-2, NLT

God is Moving: Creating a Faith-Based Community Garden

The act of gardening can teach us something about ourselves, about our interdependence with the world of nature, about the relationships between work and creativity, and about how we might begin to discern those spiritual facts that elude us in other aspects of life. Gardening can also be an expression of community and conversation—another way to say that God is with us on the earth, a way to picture God's presence with us—through the gifts of nature and gardening together.[15]

In the last few years millions of people have suddenly become passionate about growing their own food. Community gardens are springing up in church parking lots, housing projects, school playgrounds, and vacant urban blocks of land that have stood empty for years.

I believe this passion is a move of God that many of us miss out on because we have preconceived ideas about how God works. God moves through worship and revival meetings. God's spirit could not possibly be concerned about us digging a garden in our church parking lots. Or could it? God's desires to bring wholeness to all the broken and scarred parts of our world. God wants to restore relationships—to Godself, to each other, and to God's creation as well. Gardening accomplishes all of these.

---

15. Edythe Neumann, e-mail message to author, March 25, 2010.

Starting a community garden often revitalizes churches as neighbors are drawn in to participate. It also strengthens the church community and sparks new ministries that feed the hungry and teach basic skills like cooking and canning for those who have never cooked from scratch before. People often tell me they feel closer to God in the garden than they ever do in a church, which really shouldn't surprise us as humankind first communed with God is in a garden.

There are many reasons to start a church based community garden. The commonest motive is the desire to help those in need, especially during these unstable times. Others want to provide locally grown organic food for their kids and help them develop healthy eating habits. Still others want to heal our earth or create a beautiful green space where congregations and neighbors can enjoy God's creation.

A community garden is not just a place to grow food. It is a way to express our faith and interact with God and creation. I think God knows that it is in a garden that we connect most intimately to the character and ways of our Creator.

Church-based community gardens require lots of planning. Bring together a few passionate individuals who really want to see this happen. Before talking about garden logistics, discuss why you feel this is important as a church activity. What are the benefits you hope the congregation and the neighborhood will gain? How will it help people connect more intimately to each other and to God? What are the values and characteristics of God's kingdom that this garden could portray?

Jeff Littleton, who founded Five Loaves Farm, which is developing a network of community gardens on church properties in Lynden, Washington, told me:

> The garden teaches at least two key messages beyond that of vegetables or lady bugs. One is for our church: to share, to cooperate with, to relax, to enjoy each and everybody whatever faith or worldview. The other is for our community: their capturing that these "church people" can be trusted, they do live out what they say, they love us... and 'I want to know why.' Somehow, some

TO GARDEN WITH GOD

way this joint experience will transform lives and transform communities under God's care."[16]

Working together as a church congregation provides a wonderful sense of accomplishment. It also strengthens intergenerational ties as young and old work side by side, weeding, watering and planting. You may even like to designate a special area as a children's garden where kids choose what grows and when it is harvested. At our small intentional community, the Mustard Seed House we grow about 50 percent of our own vegetables. Seven-year-old Catie not only gets a chance to introduce new vegetable varieties each year, she is also my best year-round helper. A few weeks ago she practiced her newly developed writing skills making markers for our tomato seedlings.

Incorporating sacred spaces within the garden is essential. Places for people to sit and meditate, prayer walks, community gathering spaces, even the inclusion of a labyrinth are all possible ways to strengthen people's faith beyond the activities associated with food production. Early monastic communities created walled gardens that were rich with biblical imagery, often centered on an apple tree, representing both the tree of life in Genesis and the Cross of Christ. Northgate community garden in Seattle surrounds a small hill on which a labyrinth has been created as a place for meditation.

Establishing these connections between our faith and the garden are essential. In fact I am concerned that this faith based community garden movement may not be sustainable unless we learn how to connect our new found passions to our understanding of God and God's world.

Once the basic garden plan has been moved through the appropriate church organizational process, it is usually fairly easy to recruit additional help, money and in-kind donations. Every Sunday after the 10:30 am service parishioners at St. Mary's in Cadillac, Michigan, take turns weeding and tending the community

---

16. Jeff Littleton, e-mail message to author, March 25, 2010.

garden. Other churches have recruited their youth groups and retirees as volunteers or asked for donations like soil and building materials from businesses owned by church members.

Those outside the church may want to be involved too. Sonlight Community Christian Reformed Church, also in Lynden went door to door asking neighbors if they would like to participate. The Pumpkin Patch Community Garden at Millwood Presbyterian Church in Spokane Washington intentionally used Facebook and Twitter to help get the word out and had a Twitter inspired flash mob at there first big work day this year. Environmental organizations that work in the area may be interested in partnering with your efforts. Third Christian Reformed Church in Lynden partnered with AROCHA, to develop a show garden that grows new and different varieties, provides teaching to help establish other community gardens, and hands out food to neighbors.

Master Gardener associations are also usually eager to provide expert advice if not labor and skills. Local high school or community college students may also be interested in volunteering to earn their required Service Learning credits.

Another important discussion for your planning group concerns the use of garden produce. Many churches give all or part of their harvest to local food banks and other organizations that feed the marginalized. Grace Church in Old Saybrook, Connecticut, gardens a quarter acre of land and donates its produce to the local Shoreline Soup Kitchens and Pantries, helping to feed 2,000 needy families each month. In 2009 the garden provided about 17,000 lbs of produce. Other churches distribute the food amongst church members or invite neighbors to freely harvest from the garden encouraging a sense of community that goes far beyond the church congregation.

Community gardens often provide the foundation for other church related activities. Classes in gardening, cooking and preserving arise out of garden

---

17. Pat McCaughan, "Urban Farming, Edible Landscaping Helps Offset Rising Prices," *Episcopal News* (June 09, 2008).

related activities. Classes on health and nutrition, healing the earth and other environmental issues and even spiritual formation can also have their origins in such endeavors. My own venture into conducting seminars on The Spirituality of Gardening grew out of constant prodding from friends who wanted to learn more about not just how to grow vegetables but also about how to connect their experiences to their faith.

Mongomery Victory Garden in Silver Spring, Maryland, offers the following great advice for anyone contemplating starting a faith based community garden:

> Start with a small group of committed individuals, but work hard to involve the entire congregation in some way; look for ways to make the process educational, and to make connections to your faith tradition; enlist people, especially young people from the community outside the congregation; start small and do realistic planning, especially when it comes to people's crops in the beginning; keep a garden log and update the congregation throughout the process; expect surprises and have fun.[18]

Faith based community gardens, like any community project are not without their challenges. People are concerned about safety and liability issues, whether the project is sustainable for the long run, who will do the weeding and harvesting, where the water and electricity will come from. Even what to do with the sometimes overwhelming abundance that explodes over the summer can be a problem. All of these are issues that need to be discussed and planned for.

No matter how many challenges there are, nothing can take away from the deep satisfaction of getting one's hands into the earth, digging, planting and harvesting the bounty of God's good creation. Nor can they detract from the joy that engulfs as as we experience the awe inspiring generosity of a God who wants to provide abundantly for all of humankind. The garden is a place of healing, of wholeness and of deeply spiritual encounters where God restores our bodies and our spirits in a way that is truly miraculous.

---

18. Montgomery Victory Gardens, accessed August 30, 2010, at http://www.montgomeryvictorygardens.org/documents/pdf/Tips for FBCG.pdf.

Organic Gardening 101

"Listen! A farmer went to plant seed.
Some seeds were planted along the road…
Other seeds were planted on rocky ground…
Other seeds were planted among thornbushes…
But other seeds were planted on good soil and produced grain."[19]

For me, the garden has become a metaphor for life and the ways that God interacts in our lives. But as I have learned about the priniciples of organic gardening and its dynamics and interactive nature, this analogy has become even more vivid.

A good organic garden doesn't happen overnight. It requires perseverence and patience. It takes time to transform and build up soil with compost and green manure crops. It might take even longer to work out which crops grow best in which part of the garden or how to intermingle vegetables and ornamental plants to produce an overall pattern that is pleasing to the eye as well as the palate. And just when we think we have it all figured out, the weather pattern changes, and we feel as though we are back to square one. Similarly the work of transformation that God accomplishes in our lives happens over time.

---

19. Matthew 13:3-8, NIV

1. **Planning:** Probably the most important technique in good organic gardening is planning. Organic gardening is dynamic and creative, just like the God who created our gardens and is at work in our lives. So in winter, exercise this creativity with plans and ideas for the coming growing season. Mark special celebrative occasions on your calendar that you hope will be provided for out of the garden. You might want to plant an extra row of spring lettuce for your best friend's wedding or you might want to cut back on summer crops because they will fall on the ground and spoil while you are away on vacation. No one wants to come back to a zucchini that is now totally inedible.

2. **Buy the Right Tools:** The backyard gardener only needs a few tools, most of which are inexpensive
    - A shovel to prepare the soil for planting
    - A hand fork and kneeler for weeding on your knees
    - A long handled hoe for weeding larger areas
    - Pruning shears for larger bushes and plants
    - A garden hose or simple irrigation system for large areas and a watering can for pots.
    - An all purpose organic fertilizer

3. **Build Up the Soil:** The soil rather than the plant needs to be nurtured and built up. Healthy soil produces healthy plants. When I first started gardening, I wasn't concerned about whether or not my methods were organic, and like all novice gardeners, I started by fertilizing and protecting the plant rather than building up the soil. All that changed when I tried to kill some insects and ended up with a dead bird. I realized that what I sprayed on my plants had far more impact than just killing a few bugs. As I researched pesticides, I was shocked to discover how toxic they could be, not just to the bugs they were meant to kill, but also to wildlife, aquatic animals, and even people who handled them. It didn't take long to convert me to a new way of gardening.

Similarly I have become a strong advocate for growing healthy Christian communities because I have realized how essential community is to the growth of mature, fruitful followers of Christ. I am very aware of how much more rapid my Christian growth is when I am part of a strong healthy Christian community that nurtures my inner development and repels nasty pests like sin and greed that otherwise attack and destroy me.

4. **Organic Pest Control:** Organic gardening doesn't mean you have to put up with insects eating all your plants or slugs infesting your salads. Though the term essentially means not using synthetic pesticides and fertilizers, organic gardening is really far more than that. This method depends on techniques that work in cooperation with nature, encouraging natural pest control by inviting beneficial birds and insects and replenishing rather than depleting the soil by the use of compost and green manure crops. And that seems like something our creator God would be much happier with than lots of toxic substances.

5. **Use Green Manures or Cover Crops:** Planting overwintering crops like fava beans and clover can help restore nitrogen to the soil and also prevent erosion. Unfortunately, in the rhythm of my life, October, when these crops should be planted, is often a very busy travel time.

6. **Crop Rotation:** Another important technique for the avid gardener, though it is often a challenge for those of us who have limited space and even more limited sun. When the same crop is grown in the same spot year after year, it not only depletes the soil of nutrients, but it also enables nematodes and fungal pests to multiply. Like most urban gardeners with limited space, I need to compromise in this area, though I do try to rotate my major crops like tomatoes over a period of years.

7. **Watch and Listen to Your Garden:** Take note of what grew best last year and where it grew. Did you cluster plants with similar watering and fertilizer needs? Did you discover new dry or marshy spots in your garden? What new birds, insects, and small animals took up residence because

of your techniques? For example, since I planted lavendar, the bumble bees have become regular visitors busily pollinating the squash and other edibles. Consider keeping a garden journal of everything that happens.

8. **Encourage Diversity:** Variety is the spice of life for the avid backyard organic gardener. It is not just plant variety that is important, it is also wildlife diversity. An organic garden is alive with constant humming of bees, chirping of birds, and busyness of flitting butterflies. Attracting and keeping birds, insects, spiders, toads, bats, and even the earthworms and microbes is a wonderful way to get kids involved in the garden. Like us, all of God's creatures need shelter, water, and food to survive. Keeping the birdbath full, choosing nectar-producing flowers, and building bird houses and feeding logs can all encourage children to interact with and learn to love the garden at an early age.

In her delightful book *A Blessing of Toads*, nature writer Sharon Lovejoy reminds us, "A garden gives many harvests, but perhaps the most important is the one that awakens our spirits every single day. Wordsworth described it as the 'harvest of a quiet eye'."[20] What a wonderful insight into the Christian life! When we allow our spirits to be awakened each day by the presence of our loving, compassionate God, our lives give many harvests that are rich and fruitful.

---

20. Sharon Lovejoy, *A Blessing of Toads: A Gardener's Guide to Living With Nature* (New York: Hearst Books, 2004), 19.

Garden Strategies

God bless the earth and all that lives within it,
God bless the earth and all that lives upon it,
God bless the earth and all that live above it,
God bless the soil on which we live and work and make community,
In your mercy may it bring forth goodness,
May it nourish and renew the whole community who share it.[21]

All gardens—even wild gardens—need a certain amount of organization in order to flourish. We need to know not just what we would like to grow in the garden but what will flourish in our climate and soil conditions. I was delighted a few months ago to discover a great blog post that gave some great strategies to help me plan the vegetable garden. Here are Roy Stahl's suggestions:

1. **Refrigerator Method:** Open your fridge and think what has been in it over the last 12 months. What are things you will always find and what are "one-offs"? If you have a good climate for growing vegetables, this is the best method because you know you will use what you grow.
2. **Native Method:** If you already know what grows in your area, then focus on what grows well. Don't grow artichokes if you have hot summers. Don't grow carrots if you've got heavy, clay soil.

---

21. Part of this prayer is adapted from one written by Ray Simpson.

3. **Frugal Method:** Grow vegetables that are expensive at the supermarket. Think of short shelf life, high consumption veggies like lettuce, or lower production volume but delicious cherry tomatoes that can cost $3 for just a half quart!
4. **Anti-Pesticide Method:** You may want to grow certain vegetables that have the highest pesti-cide load, such as sweet bell peppers, celery, lettuce, spinach, potatoes, carrots, and green beans.
5. **Tiny Garden Method:** If you have limited space to grow, then you may find herbs and vegeta-bles that don't take up much space to be your favorites. You may also like the Square Foot Gar-dening techniques by Mel Bartholomew.[22]
6. **Squirrel Garden Method:** The opposite of the Tiny Garden Method and may require a large area. If like a squirrel with its acorns, you want to stow away vegetables for the winter, then think about setting aside garden space for storage vegetables like potatoes, onions and garlic. Think of what can be dried (beans, herbs) or canned/frozen (tomato sauce). We highly recom-mend Yin-Yang beans!
7. **Impress the Neighbors Method:** Ok, so I am guilty of doing this with our purple artichokes that grow next to the sidewalk (purple anything is a great conversation piece). Go through your seed catalogs until you say, "What the heck is that?" and then if it grows in your area, grow it in your garden. Grow it in your front yard to befuddle neighbors walking by with their dogs.[23]

As I thought about these suggestions in relation to how I viewed gardening as a spiritual discipline, I realized that there were a few other strategies I wanted

---

22. http://www.squarefootgardening.com

23. Roy and Giselle Stahl, "7 Different Strategies to Plan Your Vegetable Garden," (January 28, 2009), accessed April 22, 2009, at http://plangarden.wordpress.com/2009/01/28/7-different-strategies-to-plan-your-vegetable-garden/. Used with permission.

to include—strategies that flow directly from my faith and God's principles explained in the Levitical laws.

So to the excellent list above I would add:

8. **Garden With Friends:** I never enjoy gardening as much as I do when the other members of the Mustard Seed House community are there planting seeds too. Catie, who is seven years old, has her own garden journal as well as her own garden. A couple of years ago, she prompted us to grow celery, which is something I had never enjoyed before. But homegrown celery is wonderful. This year she is starting us on radishes and we are all excited to see the seeds sprout.

9. **Share With Neighbors:** Gardening is a way to be truly hospitable. I always start far more toma-toes, cauliflowers, and squash than I need and have found that one of the most effective ways to get to know my neighbors is to share the seedlings with them. Then of course when the squash explode and I am faced with fifty pounds of zucchini, sharing is the only way to cope. When this happens I am always reminded of the story of the children of Israel eating manna in the desert. There was always enough for everybody and if they hoarded it, then it went bad.

10. **Plant a Row for the Hungry:** There is a growing movement among backyard and community gardeners to plant an extra row specifically to give away to food banks and ministries that pro-vide for the poor and the homeless. In Leviticus, God instructs the Hebrews thus, "When you reap the harvest of your land, do not reap to the very edges of your field or gather the gleanings of your harvest. Do not go over your vineyard a second time or pick up the grapes that have fallen. Leave them for the poor and the foreigner."[24]

11. **Plant Some Unusual, Fun Varieties:** Purple cauliflowers and green toma-toes are great conversation starters, as Roy Stahl says in the Impress the

---

24. Leviticus 19:9-10, TNIV

Neighbors Method, but I'll take it one step fur-ther and say that unique vegetable varieties can lead to deep discussions about the creativity and glory of God.

12. **Don't Take Yourself Too Seriously:** As I said, I am the queen of messy gardens. I love to sit and enjoy the flowers and the fragrances, but if I worry about the fact that there are still weeds around the strawberries and snails on the lettuce then it is not nearly as enjoyable. And maybe this is just me rationalizing my way of doing things, but I cannot imagine that the God who would create animals as entertaining as a monkey or as unusual as a bumblebee could possibly take himself too seriously.

Gardening as Spiritual Practice

*Oh, Adam was a gardener, and God who made him see
That half a proper gardener's work is done upon his knees,
So when your work is finished, you can wash your hands and pray
For the Glory of the Garden, that it may not pass away!
And the Glory of the Garden it shall never pass away!*[25]

What is a spiritual discipline? I have grappled with this question a lot over the last few years as I have worked to integrate my spiritual practices with my everyday life. At one stage I posed the question on my blog: Where do you most frequently connect to God? To my surprise, the commonest answer was "in the garden," or "walking in nature."

This made me realize that I need to redefine what I mean by a spiritual discipline. It is not something that comes from a narrowly defined set of activities that revolve around church and scripture reading. I think that a spiritual practice is anything that connects us more intimately to God and God's world. Or, as Shane Tucker commented on his blog recently, "They are in effect, 'space-makers,' allowing God to meet us where we're at as He's always done right throughout

---

25. Rudyard Kipling, "The Glory of the Garden," *Eerdman's Book of Christian Poetry*, Pat Alexander, comp. (Grand Rapids, Mich.: Eerdmans Publishing, 1981), 81.

human history." Now that doesn't mean that I can do anything I want and call it a spiritual practice. What it does mean, however, is that my life needs to focus on a very clear vision of God's kingdom purposes, and everything I do needs to be interpreted by how it helps me live more deeply into that world.

So what do I mean by this? I have long believed that most people practice their spiritual disciplines within an environment of chronic randomness. They have very little idea of where they are heading, and so, even though they may read the bible regularly and pray regularly, they really do not have a clear plan as to where these practices are meant to take them and how their prayers and scripture read-ing move them along the journey. On top of that, it really restricts our understanding of spiritual disciplines to these kinds of practices.

If I really believe (and I do) that God's ultimate plan is the restoration of all things in Christ and recognize that I am called to join God in the business of this restoration, then everything I do becomes a spiritual discipline that is part of that process. I pray and I read scripture because it better equips me to participate in the work of restoration by bringing about the inner healing I need to make this possible, or by strengthening my relationship to God so that I can operate in the power of the Holy Spirit, or by drawing me closer to God's people and the world.

Gardening has becomes a spiritual discipline for me because it connects me to God and the story of God in a multitude of ways. First, like the early monks who grew gardens to re-create something of the Garden of Eden, I see in every garden a glimpse of God's transformed world in which the beauty of God's original creation is restored and there is abundant provision made for all of God's people. The intricate beauty of each fragile flower is breathtaking, and the way that God can blend together colors that you and I would only combine into a hideous mess is unbelievable.

---

26. Shane Tucker, "Matters of the Heart Pt. Two;" Nascent Narratives from the Edge of the World blog (February 13, 2009), accessed April 22, 2009, at http://wwwdreamtoday.blogspot.com/2009/02/matters-of-heart-pt-two.html.

In addition, I kneel to do many of my garden tasks. I kneel to weed, to plant seeds and seedlings, and even sometimes to harvest strawberries and other garden produce. In this position of supplication, I often find myself meditating and praying. If I am troubled by some seemingly insurmountable problem, there is no better place to try and thrash it out than on my knees in the garden. And also, if I am irritable or depressed, there is no better therapy than garden weeding.

I am not alone in this. When I posed my question about encountering God in the garden, Marla Jayne shared the following story: "I recently heard a woman talk about how she had learned that her pre-cious grandson was born with Down Syndrome and just could not calm her anxiety about it. She got up before dawn and went to work in her garden. She prayed and cried and weeded and prayed and cried and replanted, until suddenly she felt peace and knew that no matter what happened, all would be fine."[27]

God often comforts and heals our spirits as we kneel in the garden in a way that I think is truly miracu-lous. In the midst of God's creation, a healing balm of God's presence is poured out and brings us wholeness.

---

27. Marla Jayne blogs at http://marlajayne.wordpress.com.

Garbage Into Gold

*You will go out in joy
and be led forth in peace;
the mountains and hills
will burst into song before you,
and all the trees of the field
will clap their hands.*[28]

Compost is amazing stuff. Every year I spread buckets full of rich black loamy material onto my garden. Some of it comes from the local nursery, but a growing portion of it comes from our own backyard piles. Last year we added a stackable worm bin which is a great way to compost kitchen scraps which can attract rats and other vermin to your yard waste bin. The top tray is fresh food scraps covered by shredded paper that serves as bedding for the worms. Ideally the food should be in small bite-sized pieces, but that rarely happens in my bins. The worms still seem to crunch and munch their way through the scraps. When the material in the bottom level is decomposed the worms move up into fresh material and the tray is removed. While we wait for the material to decompose we can still draw off, what is called "worm tea" each week.

---

28. Isaiah 55:12, TNIV

This rich mix of nutrients is one of the best and also one of the most expensive fertilizers around—black gold indeed.

According to a Natural Lawn and Garden resource, "There are lots of ways to make good compost—the best method is the one that is most convenient for you."[29] That sounds like my kind of advice. We use what is called cool composting, which takes a little longer (6–18 months), but has the advantage of requiring very little work. All we do is add dead stuff like yard trimmings and garden waste to the bin as they become available. We water it occasionally and wait. Ideally the pile should contain an equal mix of green and brown materials, but to be honest, we rarely worry about that and we still seems to end up with decent compost. We don't even take the time to turn the pile. The bacteria, worms, bugs, and fungi all go to work, and one day we open the bin and there is this amazing sweet-smelling black gold.

What goes on in our compost pile and worm bin is truly incredible. Last week, when I lifted the lid to the worm bin, I watched the thousands of red wriggly worms diligently at work transforming our stinky food waste and garbage into fertilizer. Gone were the moldy leftovers from the fridge and the rotten potatoes that had not survived our hard frosts this year. Gone were the dead corpses of broccoli plants and discarded leaves. Gone was the smell of death and corruption. Like and unlike had blended together into something totally new. In their place was rich, black, sweet-smelling compost ready to be spread on the garden. It is the best fertilizer around, not only because it adds nutrients to the soil, but also because it improves the soil structure so that roots can grow deeper and water is better retained. Healthy, well-composted soil makes it easier to pull weeds and recycles nutrients and organic matter that helps grow trouble-free plants with less water and less problems with pests. And we get an added glow

---

29. Seattle Public Utilities, "Composting Yard and Food Waste at Home," accessed April 22, 2009, at http://seattle.gov/util/stellent/groups/public/@spu/@csb/documents/webcontent/spu01_001989.pdf, 3.

of reduced garbage bills for costly landfills.

As I contemplated this amazing transformation, I could not help but think of the ways that God trans-forms our lives. Often it is the stinky, smelly things from our past, those things we want to throw out in the garbage, that God wants to take hold of and transform into the foundations of our faith and minis-try. It is often the addictions, failures, and inadequacies of our lives that God transforms into our strengths. At least that has been the experience of my life.

Thank God for compost and worms! Thank God for the healing and trans-forming power of the gospel that can take the very worst of who we have been and transform us all into the people God intends us to be!

Winter

A Season for Quiet and Retreat

Winter Pruning

Faithful God, creator of all times and seasons,
We so easily forget that hidden within the night's dark embrace are the seeds of life.
Remind us, loving God, that when all seems dark and empty,
You are still at work strengthening roots, healing wounds, anchoring our lives.
Remind us, generous God, that when morning dawns,
It is the night's long rest that has sustained and nurtured our souls.
Keep us faithful, God, through the dark journey of life,
So that when the new dawn breaks our roots may be deep and strong.

I used to hate winter. I hate being cold, and I hate being confined to the house on the dark, dreary, rainy days in Seattle. The garden, however, has taught me to see winter in a new light. It is still dark and dreary at times, but I am aware now that even in this season, the light of God is able to shine through. In truth, there is nothing more beautiful than a cold, clear, crisp day in Seattle in the middle of winter when the sun dances on the lake near our house and the majestic snow-covered mountains shout God's glory.

Winter is a season of quiet contemplation and retreat, with occasional blinding flashes of God's sun-shine, insights of understanding that can only come in the midst of darkness. This is a time when all of nature, including human beings, slows down and longs to rest. I have already covered my tender perennials with mulch, and brought my geraniums inside so that they will survive the winter. And I have planted garlic and some new shrubs that I hope will adorn my garden next year.

I was fascinated to discover recently that shrubs planted in autumn are more likely to flourish than those planted in spring because they spend the winter sending down roots. Deep roots anchor them against storms and strong winds and enable them to draw more deeply from the water that abides deep within the soil even in times of drought.

My most profound garden lessons probably come from winter. Why, I wonder, do we prune our fruit trees in the winter when they seem so bare and vulnerable? Or probably more to the point, why does God insist on pruning our lives during the difficult winters of suffering that we all endure? Winter pruning, like autumn planting, encourages roots to go down deeper and strengthens the tree. The harder we prune, the more vigorous the spring growth will be and the greater the harvest. As I think about this I am reminded of the words of Jesus:

> I am the true vine, and my Father is the gardener. He cuts off every branch in me that bears no fruit; while every branch that does bear fruit he prunes so that it will be even more fruitful.... Remain in me as I remain in you. No branch can bear fruit by itself: it must remain in the vine. Neither can you bear fruit unless you remain in me.[1]

God often plants us in places where winter is coming or prunes us during the frigid seasons of struggle and pain, when the branches seem bare and our souls feel most vulnerable. Often the pruning is just as severe as what I inflict on my trees. If we really want to be fruitful during the seasons of harvest that God allows us, then we need to be willing to be pruned and shaped not during the times that life is good, when we can handle a little painful cutting, but during winter when we feel spring will never come again.

I think that God intends us to embrace the winter seasons of our lives as times of learning, growing, and strengthening. As Jean Vanier, founder of L'Arche communities, reflects:

---

1. John 15:1-4, TNIV

WINTER: A SEASON FOR QUIET AND RETREAT

> We must go through winters of suffering, through times when prayer is hard and people no longer attract us, but spring is not far away. A death in the family, a failure at work, a sickness which brings a new way of life, an unfaithful friend, all these are wounds to the heart that take us into a period of darkness. The darkness is important. We must learn to accept this winter as a gift from God and we will discover that the snow will melt and the flowers come up.[2]

Winters of suffering, when fully embraced, strengthen our inner being in ways that the good times can never do. But just as I hate the cold days of winter and want to run away from the dark and the rain, so I want to run away from the heartache and anguish of suffering. Yet I am coming to realize that during those seasons when life seems darkest, God is sending down spiritual roots that make it possible for me to stand firm through the otherwise overwhelming seasons of growth and harvest that may lie ahead.

---

2. Jean Vanier, *Essential Writings*, Carolyn Whitney-Brown, ed., (Maryknoll, NY: Orbis Books, 2000) 137.

Waiting for the Light

As quietly as the winter steals upon us,
the season of joy approaches.
We wait for our Redeemer,
We wait for the light of the world,
In this season of expectancy,
We wait for God's love to come in fullness.
Come in the glory or your saving light
Radiate within us and shine on our paths,
Open our eyes to your presence,
For light penetrates the darkness,
and prepares the way of the Lord.

Winter is a season for waiting, not just in the garden, but in our lives as well. In the Northern Hemi-sphere, its beginning coincides with the liturgical season of Advent during which we await the coming of the light—God's light that will be revealed at Christmas in the birth of the baby Jesus. Many of us find the shortening days of winter depressing, and as we move toward Christmas, our longing for the light intensifies. The bare branches of the trees now stripped of their leaves, reach quietly toward the light reflecting our longing.

One of my favorite seasonal traditions that seems to highlight this longing is making an Advent wreath. Its origins, though not directly related to gardening, are closely linked to those who work the land. Evidently it originated in the colder climates of northern Europe where men would remove the wheels of horse-drawn wagons just before winter set in, when snow and muddy conditions made travel difficult. The wheels were brought inside and hung in the rafters. Eventually they were deco-rated with boughs and candles, becoming this wonderful symbol of waiting for the coming of Christ. We don't just await his coming to us as a baby, we also remember his coming as a Savior to any who will receive him. And we await in breathless anticipation his second coming at the end of time, when God will make all things new.

Tom and I set up an Advent wreath on the dining room table each year. Four bright red candles around a central white candle nestle in a bed of greenery cut from the garden. At breakfast each morning, we light the appropriate candles, symbolic of the fact that Christ is our light in the darkness of the world. During the first week of Advent, only one candle is lit. Then a fresh candle is lit each week until on Christmas Day, all the candles are set alight to welcome Christ. Their brightness shines over our break-fast table throughout the twelve days of Christmas. As the candles burn brightly, we read the daily scriptures from the *Book of Common Prayer*, focusing on our anticipation of the coming of Christmas and our celebration of Christ's birth. At this busy season of the year, this short ritual helps me refocus my energy beyond the consumer culture to my faith. It brings tremendous refreshment and renewal to my spirit.

Tom and I also like to go on a prayer retreat during Advent. We get away for a couple of days to reflect on what we believe to be God's call on our lives. We review our mission statement and set goals for the next year that flow out of our sense of God's purpose for us. Prayer retreats like this have become im-portant breaks in our busy lives. They help us to keep focused on God's purposes rather than our own desires and ambitions and enable us to accomplish all that God intends for us to do. In the Southern Hemisphere, though winter has no compa-rable liturgical significance, it is still a good time to slow down and plan a retreat to contemplate the coming of the one who gives life and meaning to all we are and do.

I suspect we would all be loathe to take the wheels off our cars and decorate them in the winter, but as the garden rests in expectation of the coming of new life in the spring, we too are encouraged to slow down, to rest, and to await the coming of the light of the world.

Dreaming Big

Winter's come, grey days unfolding
Winds blow, rains freeze
Leaves fall, dancing down the street
The earth slows, prepares to rest
Beneath the gathering dark,
It slumbers down.
Dark, chill, and quiet,
Waiting, watching, hoping,
Longing for God's light to shine
To penetrate the darkness and radiate within us.
Come, true light of the world,
God's son, redeemer, savior, Lord
Come into the wintery place of our lives
And bring new life.

Winter is a time for dreaming. Straight after Christmas the seed catalogues begin to arrive, and my color-starved brain laps up the beautiful glossy photos of all that could and could not grow in my garden. I love to dream big at this season. It helps me wash away the winter blues and fills my mind with wonderful possibilities. Of course, I would need a garden ten times the size I have to plant everything that catches my eye, but it is fun to dream.

I use the square foot method of gardening made popular by Mel Bartholomew's book *Square Foot Gardening*.[3] He suggests that the best way for all of us to garden is to develop a crazy patchwork in which each square foot contains a different type of plant. Not only does this mean we can fit more in a small area, but it also makes gardens more pest-resistant. Nasty bugs may nibble through one cabbage but then run into a carrot that holds no interest for them. And hope-

---

3. Mel Bartholomew, *The Square Foot Gardener* (Emmaus, Penn.: Rodale Press, 1981).

fully they starve before they discover the next cabbage halfway down the row. In a large field that contains only a single variety of seed, once a pest gets established it can sweep through the entire crop in no time, requiring the use of vast quanti-ties of pesticides to keep it under control.

My favorite catalogues are those from organizations, like Seeds of Change[4] and Seed Savers Exchange[5], that work to preserve biodiversity and promote sustainable, organic agriculture. The genetic diversity of the world's food crops is eroding at an alarming rate. Large-scale commercial farmers and agri-businesses limit their varieties to one or two strains of any crop, which they forcably grow around the world by using vast quanitites of chemical pesticides. They work on the principal that "one size fits all." As any of us who have tried to buy clothes based on that same principal know, that never works.

The vegetable and fruit varieties getting lost in the throes of agri-business are those that have been bred and selected by local farmers over thousands of years. Each variety is genetically unique, perfectly suited for its small climatic microcosm, and has developed resistance to the diseases and pests with which it evolved. When local farmers use these locally bred varieties, they need few chemical pesticides. When they switch to the apparently higher yielding breeds encouraged by agri-businesses, they also need to buy the high priced and sometimes dangerous pesticides needed to keep the crops healthy in their environment. Plant breeders use the old varieties to breed resistance into modern crops that are constantly being attacked by rapidly evolving diseases and pests. Without these infusions of genetic diversity, food production is at risk of epidemics and infestations. And then, we need to discover new and more deadly pesticides to keep disease at bay.

Organic gardeners know that God loves diversity, and they constantly succumb to the lure of purple and green cauliflowers to compliment the more

---

4. http://www.seedsofchange.org
5. http://www.seedsavers.org

ordinary white kind. The huge array of tomatoes available really sends us wild. We dream of a summer salad resplendent with green, yellow, and red cherry tomatoes, or of lush bacon, lettuce, and tomato sandwiches made with huge slices of sweet Brandywines, the most wonderful of the heritage varieties. I am not a purist, so I do not disdain hybrid varieties, even though I know that I will never be able to save their seed. But because I only grow a couple plants of each variety each year, a packet with twenty seeds in it will last me until the seed is well past its viability date.

"How like God," I think as I dream about the patchwork-quilt garden I want to create. Human beings are meant to live together in communities of rich diversity too. When we congregate only with people who look and think alike, we may end up with a big church, but I wonder if we are susceptible to more "pests" that can easily sweep through and destroy the crops we are hoping to harvest.

To share life as God intends us to, in appreciation of the rich diversity of God's world, encourages us to willingly enter into the life journeys of brothers and sisters from across the globe. That means walking alongside people from other cultures and perspectives, learning to understand their viewpoints, being willing to share their burdens, embrace their pain, and do what we can to alleviate their suffering. We are called to show God's love by sharing our talents and resources to enable others to enter into the freedoms of Christ's kingdom.

Spring

A Season of New Life

Garden Resurrections

God planted a mustard seed
deep within my heart
A tiny grain, a kingdom presence
A hidden germ of life
Warmed by God's love it grew
Sending down its roots
A tender shoot, branches too
and in its season fruit
A harvest far beyond my dreams
increasing through the years
A miracle, a life transformed
abundant act of grace.

I never fully appreciated the Easter story until I spent my first spring in the Pacific Northwest. A profusion of glimmering new leaves in a thousand shades of green, gold, red, copper, and silver emerged from the barren branches. Shrubs and trees covered in a profusion of pink, red, and yellow blossoms overwhelmed me with their fragrance. And bulbs, thousands of them, all beautiful, pushed their fragile heads up through the chilly earth. Splashes of daffodils, sunny and golden, waved in the wind. Proud, exotic tulips in every color of the rainbow followed behind, their bold colors dancing in interlacing clusters through the garden.

In Australia, where Easter generally falls at the beginning of autumn, when the garden is dying and everything is preparing for winter, it is very hard to believe in the resurrection. But when the spring bursts forth in all its glorious new life just as we are entering the Easter season, it is not hard to imagine Christ bursting forth from the tomb as well.

The garden is a constant reminder of the Easter story. Each time I plant a tiny misshapen seed, bury it in the earth, and watch it sprout, I feel that I am participating in the death and resurrection of Christ. Jesus was very aware of this relationship too. As he expressed it, "Unless a seed of wheat falls into the ground and dies, it remains only a single seed. But if it dies, it produces many seeds."[6]

Early Celtic Christians were very aware of this. Three days before farmers sowed their seeds, they would sprinkle them with water in the name of the Father, Son, and Holy Spirit. If possible they would always plant on a Friday. The moistening had the effect of hastening the seed's growth. Friday was chosen because it was the day of Christ's death and burial. The whole process of planting was symbolic of the planting of Christ, the seed of the new world in which resurrection will come for all humankind as well as for creation.

There are other enactments of this wonderful story in the garden. The ugly, hairy caterpillar that I am most likely to squish beneath my boot because I think that it is eating my cauliflowers is another wonderful reminder of God's redemption story. If left alone it will eventually encase itself in a cocoon and emerge transformed into a moth or butterfly.

I have discovered recently that most caterpillars get a bad rap. There are only a few varieties, like the cabbage moth caterpillar, that eat my cabbages and cauliflowers and are truly destructive. Unfortunately many gardeners tend to destroy them indiscriminately, often greeting their appearance with a quick spray of insecticide. Though we love to have a garden full of butterflies, we have little tolerance for their precursors. In addition, native butterflies and caterpillars have been hit hard by pollution and the destruction of habitats. Our love of exotic plants has alarming consequences. To attract butterflies to our gardens, we need to attract caterpillars as well. And to attract the species that are native to our areas we should not just indiscriminately throw around a packet labeled "butter-

---

6. John 12:24, TNIV

fly garden." The best way to attract caterpillars and butterflies is to plant native plants that are local or endemic to where we live.

All of us are like a seed or a caterpillar waiting to be transformed by the power of Christ's resurrection into fruitful trees or beautiful butterflies that radiate the life of God's new world. But unfortunately, most of us can be just as intolerant of the untransformed state of our fellow travelers on this planet as we are of caterpillars. And often for the same reason. We do not recognize in the drug addict and the chronically ill, in the oppressed and the marginalized, the person that is just waiting to be transformed in the image of God.

What will God's kingdom look like, you might ask? No one really knows, but as I watch the transformation of my seeds into plants that provide abundant food, I catch a glimpse. God's new world is a place of abundance for all. As I watch the breathtaking beauty of a butterfly unfold, I sense how wonderful a transformation that new world that God is creating will be for all of us. God's new world is a place where the beauty of every person will be revealed. Those we love who are maimed and distorted by addictions and illnesses will be made whole, and their true nature revealed in glorious splendor. And those who have been stepped upon, oppressed, and unjustly treated because of their race, culture, gender, or social strata will be set free to become all that God intends them to be.

Birds, Spiders, and Prophets

Consider the ravens: They do not sow or reap, they have no storeroom or barn; yet God feeds them. And how much more valuable you are than birds! Who of you by worrying can add a single hour to your life? Since you cannot do this very little thing, why do you worry about the rest?[7]

For me, one of the celebrations of spring each year is when the barn swallows that nest under our eaves return. I am always quite excited when I look out our bathroom window and see them. Mum and Dad sit on the rafters and inspect their nest from last year, a nest they have come back to for several years in a row. Now the challenge is the number of offspring who also want to nest around the house. A couple of years ago, they built a nest right above our front door. By the time we realized it, (we don't use the front door much) there were already babies in it. Being splattered by bird droppings is not exactly a welcome that guests fully appreciate. This year we are hoping to move them to the backyard.

There are many benefits, however, to having these beautiful birds around. Evidently, a nesting swallow will eat up to 8,000 insects a day (yep—thousands, not hundreds). That is definitely good for the garden and a wonderful way to

---

7. Luke 12:24-26, TNIV

cut down on the wasp and mosquito population over the summer. Even if we can't manage to encourage the birds to move away from above the front door, I think that the benefits far outweigh the problems. Maybe we will just have to get umbrellas for our guests.

Natural pest control is a very important part of the garden plan, as I learned a few years ago when my broccoli was attacked by scale insects. I was sitting inside reading my garden books when I looked out to see a flock of chickadees joyfully feasting on my unwelcome guests. When I wandered out into the garden later that day I was delighted to discover that there was hardly a scale insect left. The birds had devoured them all.

There are other residents in our garden besides birds that help to keep the pests at bay. Spiders for example, another one of God's creatures, like the caterpillar, tend to be unappreciated. I must confess that growing up in Australia where we have some of the deadliest spiders in the world has given me a rather paranoid fear of them. When I lived in Sydney, I would never put my garden boots on without first shaking them against the stairs to make sure a funnel web had not crept in during the night. And I would never move a rock in the garden before kicking it over to make sure there were no red backs hiding underneath.

It is only in the last few years that I have come to appreciate these garden sentinels and tried to avoid knocking their silk-like webs into oblivion. Spider silk is one of the great wonders of the animal kingdom. That a small creature, often less than a millimeter across, can make a substance that we humans with all our technology are unable to reproduce, a substance that is tougher, stronger and more flexible than anything else we can make, is surely a humble reminder of our insignificance beside the awe-inspiring nature of God.

In E.B. White's beloved classic *Charlotte's Web*, Charlotte the spider informs her friend Wilbur the pig, "If I didn't catch bugs and eat them, bugs would increase and multiply and get so numerous they'd destroy the earth."[8] Evidently it

---

8. E.B. White, *Charlotte's Web* (New York: HarperCollins, 1952), 40.

is true. Spiders are one of the most important forms of biological pest control in the garden and can kill up to 80 percent of the nasty bugs that infest our plants. Unfortunately they are rather indiscriminate predators and will also kill butterflies, bees, and other insects that we are trying to attract.

Spiders remind me of God's prophets who were also often unappreciated and even sometimes killed because God's people did not want to hear their message. Yet throughout the history of Israel, it was they who continually "kept the pests away," rebuking God's people and challenging them to return to the values and practices that God had given to them when they entered the Promised Land. At the same time, they pointed the way forward to the coming of the Messiah and the fulfillment of God's promise of a new world of righteousness and abundance.

At the center of this wonderful vision, Ezekiel assures us God will once more live among these people and be their ruler: "I will make a covenant of shalom with them . . . and will set my sanctuary in the midst of them forever. My dwelling place will be with them; I will be their God, and they will be my people."[9]

In Isaiah 65, we are presented with what I think is the most beautiful imagery of God's shalom vision as depicted by the prophets:

> Behold I will create new heavens and a new earth. The former things will not be remembered, nor will they come to mind. But be glad and rejoice forever in what I will create, for I will create Jerusalem to be a delight and its people a joy. I will rejoice over Jerusalem and take delight in my people; the sound of weeping and of crying will be heard in it no more. No longer will there be in it an infant that lives but a few days, or an old man who dies not live out his years; . . . they will build houses and live in them; they will plant vineyards and at their fruit. No longer will they build houses and others live in them, or plant and others eat. . . . The wolf and the lamb will feed together, the lion will eat straw like the ox, but dust will be the serpent's food. They will neither harm nor destroy on all my holy mountain, says the Lord.[10]

---

9. Ezekiel 37:26-27, TNIV
10. Isaiah 65:17-25, TNIV

What a wonderful day of rejoicing and celebration that will be when we all come home to God's kingdom of shalom! What a glorious hope these prophets proclaimed to sweep us into the New Testament and herald the coming of Christ in whom God's shalom vision is fulfilled and all that was promised in the Old Testament comes into being. No wonder Isaiah calls the Messiah "the Prince of Peace [shalom]." No wonder the angels burst forth out of the spiritual realm and into our physical world at Christ's birth, proclaiming, "Peace [shalom] on earth." Just as we rejoice in heaven and earth, all rejoiced at the coming of this promised Messiah through whom all things would be made whole, reconciled, and brought into unity again.

Tomato Theology

God bless the seed we plant this day,
As it falls into the ground to grow we remember your body broken for us,
As we sprinkle it with water we remember your blood poured out for us,
We wait for its resurrection; we wait for that first green sprout of new life.

Another important rite of spring is the planting of tomatoes. There are so many wonderful varieties available, but the only way to fully experience the joy of tomato growing is by starting them from seed. In Seattle, that means beginning in early February inside on a heat mat and then keeping the seedlings under grow lights until the middle of May. At the Mustard Seed House, our enclosed front porch, which faces south, acts as a greenhouse in this season. I diligently fill my seed starters with a hundred or more tomato seeds, tantalized by the image of sweet luscious fruit I hope will crown my garden over the summer. You have no idea how much better tomatoes taste straight out of the garden. In fact I am amazed at how much better all vegetables taste when freshly picked. No wonder so few kids (and adults) like vegetables—they've never really tasted anything the way God intended it to be.

I usually start ten to twelve different tomato varieties, most of which are not available in nurseries and certainly not on the supermarket shelf. Each year I experiment with a couple of new ones that I can't resist from glossy-paged seed catalogs. Every now and then I come across a real gem—like the lime-green salad tomato I discovered a couple of years ago at Totally Tomatoes[11] and the chocolate cherry tomato from Territorial Seeds.[12] These have now become part of my regular crop, which means that the number of plants I try to cram into the garden grows every year. Some of them are in pots, like cherry tomatoes I hope will produce Seattle's earliest crop with which I can impress the neighbors. Then there are the early season varieties like Early Girl, Legend, and a new one for this year called Fourth of July, though I can't imagine it will live up to its name. These aren't as flavorful as the later varieties, but after six months without any garden tomatoes, they taste wonderful. Cherry tomatoes are on the top of my list for taster—sweet mouthfuls of flavor that we usually eat straight off the vine. If there are any left, we dry them in the dehydrator to extend that wonderful fresh grown tomato flavor throughout the year.

Our favorite tomato of all time is the heirloom Brandywine tomato, which unfortunately is one of the last to ripen. We salivate over the plants, looking forward to the day when their huge sweet and juicy fruit will grace our bacon, lettuce, and tomato sandwiches or my favorite tomato, basil, and feta cheese salad.

There are more websites out there on how to grow good tomatoes than there are tomato varieties, so I will not deign to give my less-than-expert advice on the subject. There are also new gimmicks each year to help us grow better tomatoes—red mulch that is supposed to increase productivity by 20 percent, color-coordinated spiral supports, and this year's upside-down planters that promise pest-free crops. Maybe it's my cynical nature, but I suspect that many of these innovations do as little to help our toma-toes as all the new ideas on how to grow our faith do for us. I recently discovered, however, that indoor tomato seedlings need exercise to strengthen their stems and make them sturdier. So it helps to

---

11. http://www.totallytomato.com
12. http://www.territorialseed.com

wave your hand over the top of the plants a few times a day to simulate the wind. This is another good faith analogy as well, I think. All of us need winds of adversity that strengthen our faith and make us strong and mature.

There is no way that any store-bought tomato can ever taste as good as one plucked and eaten straight from the garden. In fact, most supermarket tomatoes have little if any real tomato flavor. Not only have they sat on the shelf for several days before being sold, they have probably also been picked green be-fore the sun and rich soil have had a chance to feed the flavor and nutrients into them for which toma-toes are renown. And then they are gassed so that they look ripe and pumped with chemicals to pre-serve their perfect appearance for as long as pos-sible. These are what I call "pretend" tomatoes, plastic facsimiles that look real on the outside, but inside, they are green and tasteless.

I think that growing tomatoes bears a lot of resemblance to the way we learn theology and practice Christian discipleship. For many of us, our theology and the way we practice our faith looks a little like supermarket tomatoes. We look pretty good on the outside—ripe and ready to be eaten—but inside, we are still green and immature. And like most of our store-bought tomatoes, supermarket faith is of-ten old, stale, and past its prime, or else it has been pumped up with artificial chemicals to keep it look-ing fresh and tasty. It's not surprising that our faith doesn't have any flavor, and even though it may last forever, it just doesn't have much attraction for others who are craving that real tomato flavor and want to bite into a spirituality that is sweet, juicy, and tasty.

What do I mean by this? Well, most of us learn theology by sitting down in chairs and having people yak at us. It might get some information into our heads, but it definitely does not get God's principles into our hearts. To be honest, I think it is the most boring and uninteresting way to learn anything. The only way that God's principles will get into our hearts is if we put them into practice. I often tell people that I learned my theology in the refugee camps in Thailand; that is where I first really had to live what I believed. That was where I really learned to taste and appreciate the rich sweetness of Christian faith hidden deep within the Bible. And I continue to learn more about the wonder of Christian faith through interacting with people from other cultures and perspectives. I read somewhere once that the early Christians felt privileged to live in a non-Christian society because they believed it was through their interactions with people outside the faith that they learned more about God. Now we think we learn best from people who think exactly the same way we do, and I suspect that explains why our theological perspectives are often regarded as old, stale, and full of superfluous additives—a little like the produce we buy in the supermarket.

Bacon, Lettuce, and Tomato Sandwich a la Tom Sine

Take 2 slices of good, crusty Italian bread and spread it with mayonnaise, mustard, or butter. Fry pieces of lean bacon and drain off the fat on paper. Place the bacon on one slice of bread and top it with tasty cheese. Place under the broiler until the cheese is melted. Top with slices of sweet onion, avocado, let-tuce, and large slices of Brandywine tomatoes. Pepper and salt to taste and place the remaining slice of bread on top. Enjoy!

Basil, Tomato and Feta Cheese Salad

1 cup fresh basil, chopped

2 cups of several tomato varieties of all different shades (red, yellow, green, chocolate), chopped

1 cup sweet onion, chopped

1 cup feta cheese, crumbled

½ cup kalamata olives, chopped

Mix ingredients together and serve with an oil and balsamic vinegar dressing.

Oven-Dried Cherry Tomatoes in Herbed Oil

When we first started processing tomatoes, I did not have a dehydrator, but I quickly realized that there was no way we could eat all the delicious cherry tomatoes our vines were producing while they were still fresh. I also knew that there was no better way to preserve that fresh tomato taste than by drying them. Oven drying is not as economical as using a dehydrator, but for small quantities of tomatoes, it is a much easier solution.

NOTE: It is important to make sure that tomatoes are throughly dried before packing them into jars. If you are using roma rather than cherry tomatoes, you can reduce the drying time by sprinkling them with salt and allowing them to stand cut-side-down on paper towels for at least an hour before placing them in the oven. Herbs and garlic should be dried until crisp.

50 cherry tomatoes, halved
4 cloves garlic, thinly sliced
8 fresh basil leaves
4 sprigs fresh thyme
8 sage leaves
2 cups olive oil

Place tomatoes cut side up on wire racks over cookie sheets. Bake in a very slow oven (250F, 120C) for 6 to 8 hours, or until tomatoes are dry. Turn and rearrange several times during drying. Place herbs and garlic on racks and bake for the last 20 to 30 minutes. Pack tomatoes, garlic, and herbs into pint- or liter-sized sterilized jar. Pour in enough oil to cover completely, and seal immediately. A boiling water bath is not necessary. The remaining oil can be used in salad dressings as you use tomatoes.

Summer

A Season for Growth

Growing God's Way

So neither the one who plants nor the one who waters is anything, but only God, who makes things grow. The one who plants and the one who waters have one purpose, and they will each be rewarded ac-cording to their own labor. For we are God's co-workers; you are God's field, God's building.[13]

Summer is a wonderful season in the garden. All the backbreaking work of turning the soil and getting down on our knees to weed and plant seems to be behind us. Not that the weeding stops, and there are other tedious chores like deadheading flowers and watering that need to continue diligently for the summer garden to flourish. The hot, dry days of summer, however, are essentially a respite for gardeners and should provide ample opportunity to sit back, relax, and watch everything grow.

I love to wander around the garden early in the morning, admiring my rapidly expanding zucchini and the beans that shoot out foot-long tendrils overnight. Sometimes I feel that if I watch closely enough, I will actually be able to see them grow.

---

13. 1 Corinthians 3:7-9, TNIV

Vigen Guiroian reminds us in his delightful little book *Inheriting Paradise*, "The fruit of the garden is not restricted to what we eat. Every garden lends something more to the imagination—beauty."[14] I am very aware of this as I sit on the bench in a sunny secluded part of the garden feasting my eyes on its beauty, admiring the flowers opening in breathtaking hues around me—velvety purple, yellow, and mauve salpiglossis, silk-like poppies, Zulu daisies with white petals radiating out from feathery black center, red and white bell-shaped penstemons, bright yellow marigolds, and multicolored snapdragons, daylilies, and nasturtiums, all alive with bees and butterflies. In the vegetable garden, the scarlet runner beans are resplendent with bright red flowers. Yellow, white, and green zucchini are multiplying. The tomatoes are ripening to shades of red, gold, green and chocolate and the eggplants are turning a bright purple.

The fact that this season of comparative inactivity is exactly when everything is growing most rapidly should remind me that though I have done the planting and watering, it is God who has done the growing and made everything flourish. Unfortunately, unless I take the time to relax and reflect, which this season beckons me to do, I rarely think about that. Actually, the problem goes much deeper. I grumble when the harvest is late or less than I expected, but take for granted the faithfulness of a God who has created such an incredible variety of luscious flavors for us to savor and colors for us to feast our eyes upon. I am overwhelmed by the fifty pounds of squash that suddenly appear when the weather warms, but I rarely give grateful acknowledgment to God, who provides so lavishly that I must be generous and share with others unless I want to throw away rotten fruit and vegetables.

Even worse, when my garden is successful, I tend to take all the credit for it and rarely acknowledge the wonder of God's creative presence in the midst of what I am doing. We even call gardening experts "Master Gardeners" as though

---

14. Vigen Guiroian, *Inheriting Paradise: Meditations on Gardening* (Grand Rapids, Mich.: Eerdmans Publishing, 1999), 14.

they are the ones responsible for the beauty and richness of what is created.

Acknowledging that everything in my garden comes from God, belongs to God, and is sustained by God is a humbling and often difficult challenge. Nothing in my garden would even germinate and burst into life, let alone grow, without God's creative and nourishing presence. What goes on in a garden is, I believe, as miraculous as any of the miracles that Jesus performed. The fact that a tiny seed germinates beneath the earth and leaps high into the air unfurling green leaves and long slender stems that support the crowning glory of fragrant blossoms is awe-inspiring, yet something I rarely acknowledge.

In my life, I can easily suffer from the same problem. I like it when people praise me for the articles and liturgies I write, and I begin to feel that I am the one who has done all the work. I can so easily claim what God is growing and the resultant harvest as my own and ignore the One who has sustained me, nurtured me, and made it possible for me to flourish and be fruitful.

What a wonderful revelation of the nature of God summer can be! Just as we must relax and take time to reflect on the wonder of God in the garden, so we must take time to reflect on God's constant activity in our lives. To fully appreciate the wonder of what God accomplishes in and through us, we must relax, sit quietly, and breathe in the deep fragrance of God's presence. Only then will we see growth and harvest from God's perspective and give glory to the God whose loving presence permeates our entire world.

Viewing God's work in this way is an incredibly liberating experience. We no longer need to take on the burden of saving the world, and we don't need to kill ourselves trying to heal everyone who is sick or set all the oppressed free. Our job is to plant the seeds God gives us to plant, add water and fertilizer, and sit back and let God do the work.

Companion Planting

You are a garden locked up, my sister my bride;
you are a spring enclosed, a sealed fountain.
Your plants are an orchard of pomegranates with choice fruits,
with henna and nard, nard and saffron, calamus and cinnamon,
with every kind of incense tree, with myrrh and aloes and all the finest spices
You are a garden fountain, a well of flowing water streaming down from Lebanon.[15]

Many people think that all there is to organic gardening is doing away with pesticides and herbicides. There is far more to it than that, however. It is a whole inter-connected process that relies on insects, birds, compost, shade, sun, and "companion planting" to encourage beneficial insects, deter pests, and enrich the soil.

Companion planting is not a new idea. According to Seeds of Change,

> There is evidence of farmers using these same techniques dating back to ancient Roman times. Many people are familiar with the idea of planting the "Three Sisters, a Native American technique that combines corn, squash, and beans. These are time-tested planting methods that some dismiss as old wives tales. They would rather plant in organized, monoculture plots that tend to

---

15. Song of Solomon 4:12-15, TNIV

have the same appearance as different color cars parked in a mall parking lot.[16]

Planting a single crop ensures dependence on pesticides, but developing an inter-related natural envi-ronment that is conducive to birds, bees, and small animals provides a peaceful retreat for family and friends as well as providing delicious food for the table.

Here is my adaptation of Seeds of Change's suggestions:

1. **Mix up your crops.** If like me, you grow lots of tomatoes and cauliflowers. It is best to grow large crops in small groups in various sections of the garden. I love to grow flowers and vegetables mixed together too, and so I am always looking for colorful vegetable varieties, like bright lights chard and flowering kale, that look good in my flower borders. Herbs, like sage, rosemary, and oregano, are others that can take pride of place in any flower garden. Also, inter-planting marigolds throughout your main vegetable plots is not only attractive, but the stench can deter pests and even reduce nematodes. Another must for any garden is sweet basil. Not only is it a wonderful culinary herb, but it also helps repel aphids, mites, and mosquitoes. It can even act as a fungicide. I also recently discovered that planting cole crops in a bed of crimson clover confuses the cabbage moths and stops them from laying eggs on your prize plants.

2. **Use row covers.** These lightweight covers are a godsend in our part of the country. They not only allow me to plant a couple of weeks earlier because they protect greens and brassicas from unexpected frosts, but they also protect from insects. I first discovered row covers after a disastrous year in which I lost all my broccoli to root maggots. With row covers I don't lose a single plant.

---

16. Kelle Carter, "Companion Planting: So Happy Together!" *The Cutting Edge*, no. 55, (April 2006), accessed April 22, 2009, at http://www.seedsofchange.com/enewsletter/issue_55/companion_planting.aspx.

3. **Provide refuge for beneficials.** Create habitats in your garden for toads, lizards, snakes, spiders, birds, and insects that prey on pests. Provide birdbaths and bird feeders and plant nectar-bearing and fruit-bearing plants that insects and birds will all delight in.
4. **Know your weeds.** I used to feel guilty because of all the weeds that popped up in my garden before I had a chance to get down on my knees and get rid of them. Now I realize that many of these are native plants that attract local beneficial organisms. I still may not want them dominating my garden, but a few are a great advantage.
5. **Use organic pesticides as little as possible.** It has been a long time since I used any form of pesticide in my garden. I have found that being tolerant of a few pests and being willing to lose an occasional plant to predators is well worth the satisfaction of knowing that I am not using any harmful chemicals in the garden. The fact that pesticides are natural does mean they are not toxic to humans, animals, or beneficial insects like butterflies and bees.

Plants need each other to thrive and so do we. Just as companion planting of different crops can be beneficial to all, so can "companion planting" in our life and faith. Unfortunately in our highly individualistic society, we rarely consider the importance of those who walk alongside us and tend to act as though all the resources we need to be good Christians can come from within ourselves.

We are meant to journey together with others who can protect us from the pests that would destroy our faith and provide support to strengthen us when we are young and weak or when we are blown by wind and storm. Companions also help provide nourishment—the food and fertilizer grow our faith and keep us walking on the journey towards God and God's kingdom. They pray for us when we are down and encourage us when we are afraid. There is no way we can walk the journey of faith without their companionship and love.

Watering: Baptizing the Garden

Jesus answered, "Everyone who drinks this water will be thirsty again, but whoever drinks the water I give him will never thirst. Indeed, the water I give him will become in him a spring of water welling up to eternal life." The woman said to him, "Sir, give me this water so that I won't get thirsty and have to keep coming here to draw water."[17]

One of the major tasks of summer is watering. "Smart watering means more than just lower water bills. It means healthier gardens. Watering too much or too little produces weak plants that are susceptible to pests and disease. Learn to give plants the right amount of water for healthy growth and to apply it so that every drop counts."[18] Most vegetables need about one inch of water per week at the beginning of summer and two inches in the hottest months.

When I first started vegetable gardening I used to water all of my plants by hand. This was a great way to get me out into the garden each day, and I loved to watch the sun sparkle on the stream that cas-caded from the hose onto my plants.

---

17. John 14:13-15, NIV

18. Seattle Public Utilities, "Saving Water Partnership: Smart Watering," accessed April 22, 2009, at http://www.seattle.gov/util/stellent/groups/public/@spu/@csb/documents/webcontent/smartwate_200311261701453.pdf.

It was rather wasteful, however, and it soon became obvious to me that this was neither the most efficient nor the most effective way to water.

Drip or soaker hoses are probably the best and usually the least expensive for vegetable gardens. They supply water directly to the soil without wastefully spraying paths. They also reduce plant diseases that are spread by soil that is splashed onto foliage. Covering soaker hoses with about two inches of organic mulch also increases the soil's water holding capacity and helps conserve moisture during periods of drought by reducing the amount of moisture lost through evaporation. Mulches also maintain uniform levels of soil moisture, which is important in preventing blossom-end rot on peppers and tomatoes.

There is a growing awareness among many gardeners that water is precious and needs to be conserved. Long-term droughts in Australia and California, combined with the pressure of increasing populations in places where water is scarce, have us constantly looking for new water-saving techniques. Use of grey water and rainwater are two approaches that have a lot of promise.

In the last few years, as many of us have become aware of the wastefulness of our water habits, rain barrels that collect runoff from roof gutters have become very fashionable. They come in all shapes and stylish designs for the fashion-conscious gardener, but many hold only fifty to seventy-five gallons of water, which hardly makes a dent in consumption. Much larger water storage units are also available, but can be unsightly additions to garden decor. The HOG tank, designed by Sydney architect Sally Dominguez, excites me most. It stores water in small spaces against walls and under houses and can hold close to 400 gallons of water.[19] I am hoping that we will be able to invest in one of these rainwater hogs in the next year or so.

Gray water is untreated, reused household water from laundry, dishes, and the bath. It is legal to use in California, but not in some other states because it can harbor harmful bacteria and spread disease. Confirm gray water use with

---

19. http://www.rainwaterhog.com

your local public utilities department. It is not much use in the vegetable garden because it should be used only on established plants such as hardy ornamental perennials. Unfortunately rain water may be suspect in some places too. Roofing materials, such as asphalt or treated wood, and lead gutters can contaminate harvested roof water and should not be used for potable water purposes. Rainwater harvested from rooftops of large cities like San Francisco can also carry atmospheric pollutants and should be used wisely on tender edible plants.

Most of us water our gardens with little thought for the clear, refreshing precious liquid that flows from our hoses and down into the soil to sustain our thirsty plants unless we are in the grip of a drought or live in one of the more arid parts of the world. And we think even less about those who live constantly on the edge of life because of water scarcity. Tragically there are about one billion people around the world who are in danger of death every day because of lack of access to clean water. Millions of others suffer from illnesses that are borne by polluted water. Some people believe that as the world's population increases, the wars of the future will be over water rather than land.

Vigen Guroian points out that water is the lifeblood of the garden and of all creation. Without water, not only would our gardens die, but we would too. Water is also the element of baptism. It symbolizes our death, burial, and resurrection with Christ and offers the possibility of rebirth and the hope of a renewed creation. As Christians, we commit ourselves through the water of baptism to resist evil and affirm our new life in Christ. Guroian suggests that each time we water the garden, we should recognize that "we tend not only the garden that we call nature but also the garden that is ourselves, insofar as we are constituted of water and are born anew of it."[20]

I wonder what difference it would make if each time we went outside on a dry and thirsty day to water we were reminded of our baptism or of the resurrection of Christ. Perhaps it would remind us of those in our world who are as

---

20. Guroian, *Inheriting Paradise*, 9.

thirsty as our plants. Or perhaps, more profoundly, each act of watering would become a sacred act that connected us to the wonder of Christ's life and the power of the resurrection.

Summer Feasting Recipes

Chocolate Zucchini Muffins

This is another of my favorite zucchini recipes which I freeze for unexpected times of hospitality. I of-ten make them in mini muffin pans which not only makes them go further but also means those con-cerned about their weight don't feel that they have sinned too drastically.

½ c. canola oil
¾ c. brown sugar, firmly packed
2 eggs
2 tsp vanilla extract
½ c. yogurt
1½ c. whole wheat flour
1 c. all-purpose flour
4 Tbsp cocoa powder
2 tsp baking soda
1 tsp baking powder
½ tsp cinnamon
2 c. zucchini, finely grated
1 c. chocolate chips
¼ c. pecans

Preheat oven to 325°F. Line two muffin pans with papers. In a large bowl, mix oil and sugar until creamy. Add eggs, vanilla extract, and yogurt. Blend well. In a separate bowl, mix together flour, cocoa powder, baking soda, baking powder, and cinnamon. Add to the butter mixture and stir by hand to combine. Add grated zucchini, chocolate chips, and pecans and stir well. Spoon the batter evenly into the pans, filling each paper 2/3 full, and bake for about 20 minutes for standard muffins or 10 minutes for mini muffins, until a toothpick inserted in the center comes out clean or they spring back when lightly touched. Makes about 24 muffins.

Zucchini, Oatmeal, and Berry Breakfast Muffins

This is one of my favorite and most useful zucchini recipes. I make them in large quantities over the summer and autumn. When we travel, we pull a couple out of the freezer for a nutritious and inexpen-sive breakfast. Or, if unexpected guests arrive, they are wonderful to serve with a cup of tea. They have comparatively little sugar in them so if you want a sweeter muffin just add more sugar or some

- 2 c. whole wheat flour
- 2 c. all-purpose flour
- 4 c. rolled oats
- 1½ c. brown sugar
- 2 tsp baking soda
- 4 tsp baking powder
- 4 tsp cinnamon
- 4 c. grated zucchini, or other summer squash (or 2 c. zucchini, plus 2 c. carrots, grated)
- 1 c. pumpkin or sunflower seeds
- 1 c. dried cranberries or fresh berries from the garden
- 1 c. pecans, chopped
- 1 c. applesauce
- 1 c. vegetable oil
- 4 eggs, lightly beaten
- 1 c. yogurt
- 2 tsp vanilla extract
- 2 over-ripe bananas, mashed

honey.

Preheat oven to 350°F and grease muffin cups. In a large bowl, sift together the flour, oats, sugar, bak-ing soda, baking powder, and cinnamon. Stir in the zuc-chini, pumpkin seeds, cranberries, pecans, and applesauce. In a separate bowl, whisk together the oil, eggs, yogurt, vanilla, and bananas. Add this mixture to the flour mixture, stirring the batter until just combined. Spoon the batter into greased cups. Bake for 15 to 20 minutes for mini muffins and 25 to 30 minutes for regular muffins, or until springy to the touch. Let muffins cool in tins and turn them onto a wire rack. Makes 45 to 50 muffins.

Quinoa Tabbouleh Salad

I love to experiment with new grains. Quinoa is one that has caught my attention because it is high in protein. It is also good for those that are intolerant of gluten. I also find that this salad stores well, so if you are going away for a couple of days, you can make it ahead just keeping the dressing separate until an hour before you want to serve it.

2 c. quinoa
2 lbs. tomatoes, chopped
1 large cucumber, chopped
2 small yellow zucchini, chopped
2 med. sweet onions, chopped
2 c. parsley, coarsely chopped
½ c. fresh mint, coarsely chopped
¾ c. olive oil
¾ c. lemon juice
1 clove garlic, crushed

Bring 4 cups of water to a boil. Add quinoa and cook covered for 15 minutes. Turn off and let stand. Fluff with a fork and allow to cool. Add tomatoes, cucumber, squash, onion, parsley, and mint. Mix well. Add remaining ingredients and mix again. Let stand for at least an hour before serving.

Citrus and Mint Iced Tea

I make this tea throughout the summer. It is both refreshing and thirst-quenching, and uses some of the garden produce. I am hoping that when my seaberry bushes start producing I will be able to substitute their juice for the orange juice. If you are concerned about using local ingredients, you may also like to substitute lemon verbena for the lemon juice.

8 tsp loose-leaf black tea, or 8 strong teabags
1 large handful fresh mint
8 c. boiling water
1 c. orange juice
½ c. lemon juice
1 orange, thinly sliced
1 lemon, thinly sliced
1 lime, thinly sliced
1 L ginger ale (or use homemade ginger beer if available)

Put tea and mint in a glass or ceramic pot. Pour in the boiling water and steep for 30 minutes. Strain and refrigerate. Pour into a large pitcher. Add lemon and orange juice. Add orange, lemon, and lime slices. Add ginger ale and serve with ice cubes.

SUMMER: A SEASON FOR GROWTH

Autumn

A Season of Overwhelming Abundance

Pumpkins Don't Leave Holes

You care for the land and water it; you enrich it abundantly.
The streams of God are filled with water to provide the people with grain,
for so you have ordained it.
You drench its furrows and level its ridges;
you soften it with showers and bless its crops.
You crown the year with your bounty, and your carts overflow with abundance.[21]

Autumn is a bittersweet season in which the gay abandon of annuals shouting out their last joyous spectacle of color is tempered by the slowing pace of ripening fruit and the gathering frenzy of animals preparing for their winter rest. For us also there is no more time for drowsy dawdling while we idly reflect on God's beauty. It is time to get back to the real work of harvesting, canning, drying, and storing. It is also time to dig new beds, plant new shrubs, and cover the tender plants we hope will survive the winter freeze.

Autumn is a harvest season, when God's generous bounty is lavished upon us in such an overwhelming fashion that we cannot but believe in a God who wants to provide abundantly for all humankind. Most years at the Mustard Seed House, we harvest about 200 pounds of tomatoes, 100 pounds of squash, and copious quantities of lettuce, Asian greens, and Swiss chard of which I usually lose

---

21. Psalm 65:9-11, NIV

track before they reach my records. There are also green and dried beans hanging from long, entwined vines, blueberries and strawberries, and the more exotic experiments—sunberries, cape gooseberries, and seaberries. I am slowly replacing ornamental shrubs with others that are both ornamental and food producing. Our trees already provide around 200 pounds of apples, 40 pounds of pears, and 30 pounds of peaches. The cherries, however, have yet to grace us with their generosity. Hopefully one day we will also enjoy pineapple guavas, moon berries, and wolf berries, which our local Raintree Nursery assures me should thrive in this area.

"Where did this thing come from?" Michael Pollan asked in his book *Second Nature* after he picked a 30-pound squash from his garden. There was no hole, after all, left behind in the garden that suggested the plant had converted 30 pounds of soil into fruit. Nor do my apple trees sink into the ground because they have given away 200 pounds of apples and are left perched on the edge of a crater. Pollan concluded, "That they're not [leaving holes], it seems to me, should be counted something of a miracle. . . . It is, in other words a gift."[22]

The most powerful message conveyed to us by the harvest is that God's creation is an amazing and miraculous example of sustainability, out of which our Creator is constantly gifting us with all that we need for life. What a contrast to the way that we tend to operate! For example, in his book *Green Revolution*, Ben Lowe talks about the devastation caused by coal mining in the Appalachian states. Evidently three million pounds of explosives are used every day in West Virginia alone to blow off the tops of mountains to access coal for our electricity. As you can imagine, that really does leave some big craters, destroying not just the environment, but also the health of the people who live there.

Once we recognize that God is the initiator of sustainability, perhaps we too can become creative inventors of sustainable systems. Solar power and wind farms, which draw from God's gifts of wind and sun, are both viable ways to

---

22. Michael Pollan, *Second Nature: A Gardener's Education* (New York: Grove Press, 1991) 143.

produce electricity without leaving holes in the ground. If we observe the world around us as a gift from God, we start to see that hidden in many aspects of God's creation are lessons for sustainability.

I have always been intrigued by biological design and was fascinated recently to discover the science of biomimicry. Biomimicry studies models found in the natural world and imitates or takes inspiration from them to help solve problems humankind encounters in society. I am intrigued by its potential for leading us to God's sustainable solutions.

The core idea of biomimicry is that for millions of years nature has grappled with the same problems we face now and came up with solutions that not only work, but also sustainable for the long term as well. According to Janine Benyus, the major proponent of this science, "Nature's design genius has led to the creation of bat-inspired ultrasonic canes for the blind, synthetic sheets that collect water from mist and fog as desert beetles do, and paint that self-cleans like a lotus leaf. Little plastic-film patches have been designed using adhesive-less gecko-foot technology, so that carpet tiles can be stored in a big roll, but also easily removed. Equally promising, we'll soon make solar cells like leaves, super tough ceramics that resemble the inner shells of abalone, and underwater glue that mimics the natural as forests."[23]

One example that really intrigues me is the discovery that peacock feathers contain only one pigment—the brown pigment *melanin*. The incredible array of "colors" we see is structural. Directional layering of the feather's *keratin* protein combines with the melanin background causing light to refract in such a way that we see color. Inspired by this design, a Japanese company has created reusable display signs whose surface is structurally altered through exposure to ultraviolet light. These signs can be continually reused and imprinted with new images, eliminating the need to manufacture new signs or use toxic waste.

---

23. Amory B. Lovins, "Janine Benyus," *Time Magazine*, accessed April 22, 2009, at http://www.time.com/time/specials/2007/article/0,28804,1663317_1663319_1669888,00.html.

John Todd researched wetland filtration after asking the question, "How does nature clean water?" This inspired the development of a wastewater treatment system that employs bioreactors with communities of organisms that use the waste input as nutrients, digesting them and in the process purifying the water. The water released is often cleaner than city water.[24]

Perhaps it is time that we all learned from the harvest and started to invest in God's ways of sustainability.

---

24. John Todd Ecological Design, "About Us," accessed April 22, 2009, at http://www.toddecological.com/company/

Harvest of Plenty

Remember this: Whoever sows sparingly will also reap sparingly, and whoever sows generously will also reap generously. Each of you should give what you have decided in your heart to give, not reluc-tantly or under compulsion, for God loves a cheerful giver.... now he who supplies seed to the sower and bread for food will also supply and increase your store of seed and will enlarge the harvest of your right-eousness. You will be rich in every way so that you can be generous on every occasion and through us your generosity will result in thanksgiving to God.[25]

The summer and autumn harvests can be overwhelming in their generosity. This awe-inspiring generosity is indeed a gift from God, and creation rejoices in praise and thanksgiving to the one who gives all things life. In this season, the squash are slowing down, but are still setting more fruit than I know how to cope with. The tomatoes hang in tempting juicy red, yellow, and green clusters from the vines. And those beautiful scarlet runner flowers have given way to long slender and delicious green beans. Some have hidden themselves so well amongst the foliage that they are fattening into meaty pods speckled with black and purple.

Much of what comes out of the garden will be dried, canned, and stored for later usage. Some will be shared with friends and neighbors or with the local

---

25. 2 Corinthians 9:13, NIV

food banks and homeless shelter. All in all, it is a joyous and enriching season that has much to teach us about the ways of God.

First, it mirrors the overwhelming generosity of God, which does indeed provide enough for our own needs and an abundance to give away and share. It is as miraculous as the feeding of the five thousand with the loaves and fishes. It is as generous and rich as the most magnificent banquet ever set before a king. It is as satisfying as any accomplishment of our own efforts.

Second, it encourages neighborliness and hospitality as we recognize that there is no way that we can consume God's bounty on our own. And if we hold on to it too long, it goes bad and spoils. God doesn't seem to believe in hoarding. God likes to provide what we need when we need it, which has the added advantage of keeping us dependent on God and not on our own abilities. That of course reminds me of the manna with which God fed the Israelites in the desert. If they gathered too much and tried to hoard it, then it spoiled too.

There are a growing number of organizations, both Christian and not, that are tapping into this overwhelming abundance of God to provide for those at the margins. Here in the Seattle area, one of these is called Lettuce Links. It encourages people to become self-sufficient by growing their own food and also links P-Patch gardeners with food banks and meal programs. They will even provide volunteers to harvest fruit from neighborhood backyards. Lettuce Links is part of a larger community organization called Solid Ground which works to overcome poverty in the Seattle area. [26]

Part of God's plan has always been the sharing of our abundance with those at the margins. The Levitical laws about leaving the gleanings for the poor and sharing with the hungry are not about charity, but rather about hospitality. Hospitality has always been an important priority for God's people. According to theologian Christine Pohl:

---

26. http://www.solid-ground.org/Programs/Nutrition/Lettuce/Pages/default.aspx

> Hospitality . . . is a concrete expression of love—love for sisters and brothers, love extended outward to strangers, prisoners, and exiles, love that attends to physical and social needs. Within acts of hospitality needs are met, but hospitality is truncated if it does not go beyond physical needs. Part of hospitality includes recognizing and valuing the stranger or guest.[27]

Christians of the Celtic tradition in the fourth century believed hospitality was not only meant to be a custom in their homes, they believed it was also a key into the kingdom of God. The guest house, or hospitium, often occupied the best site within a monastic community, and though the monks might live on bread and water, visitors were often lavishly provided with the richest of food and the best of wine—symbols of the abundance of the kingdom of God. To offer hospitality was seen as receiving Christ into their midst and fulfilling the law of love.

The monastery at Derry is said to have fed a thousand hungry people each day. Brigit, who presided over the monastery at Kildare, often made butter for visitors. Tradition has it that when churning the butter, Brigit would make thirteen portions—twelve in honor of the Apostles and an extra one in honor of Christ, which was reserved for guests and the poor.

---

27. Christine Pohl, *Making Room: Recovering Hospitality as a Christian Tradition*, (Grand Rapids, Mich.: Eerdmans Publishing, 1999), 31.

Walk Through the Garden Soup

*There is a time for everything,
and a season for every activity under heaven.*[28]

A couple of years ago I read a fascinating book on the art of winter gardening in the Pacific Northwest called *Gardening Under Cover: A Northwest Guide to Solar Greenhouses, Cold Frames, and Cloches* by William Head. I was inspired by the thought of salads fresh from the ground in the middle of winter and knew that I would be the envy of my friends and neighbors. October arrived, however, and I didn't plant a single seed. I was too busy harvesting and processing apples, tomatoes, and the other overflowing abundance that always overwhelms me at the end of the harvest season. My body was also slowing down, telling me that it was time to prepare for winter's season of inactivity and retreat. I just did not have the energy to start another crop.

At first I felt guilty. After all I am a product of a culture that tells me that there is never time to slow down or rest. Every day is meant to be more productive

---

28. Ecclesiates 3:!, NIV

AUTUMN: A SEASON OF OVERWHELMING ABUNDANCE

than the day before, and when our bodies want to slow down, we just crank up the pace, add a few more vitamins, a little caffeine, or other stimulants and keep moving. We have no sense of seasonality in our lives. Strawberries and tomatoes in winter, pears and apples in spring, oranges and beets in summer all tell us that we can have anything that we want whenever we want it. We have no concept of the fact that there are meant to be seasons for planting, growing, and harvesting, followed by seasons of rest.

Fortunately, a growing number of people around the world are convinced that eating what is in season locally is good both for us and for our planet. They are also working to convert the rest of us. Supporting locally owned businesses such as farmers' markets and community supported agriculture programs (CSAs) generates twice as much income for the local economy. Even if we eat organic food regularly, when it has travelled halfway around the world, the environmental damage that its transportation creates outweighs the benefits of buying organic.[29] In addition, farmers catering to a local market, like those of us who grow our own vegetables, can grow a richer assortment of vegetables because they can grow varieties that deteriorate rapidly when transported long distances.

The light, refreshing salad greens of summer are perfect for that season, but as the temperatures get colder, we need a different kind of fuel. We need foods that provide sustained energy, and generate warmth. And guess what—these are the foods that are available over the winter. Sweet potatoes and yams, acorn and other squashes, cabbages and cauliflowers can be picked and stored before the first frost. If you choose your varieties properly, you should have a good supply for nutritional soups throughout the winter. Root vegetables, such as carrots and beets, and others like leeks, broccoli, kale, and collard greens may even survive in the garden until you are ready to use them. Nuts and seeds like dried beans provide a wonderful supplement to these nutritious foods.

---

29. "Local Food 'Greener Than Organic'," *BBC News*, March 2, 2005, accessed April 22, 2009, at http://news.bbc.co.uk/2/hi/science/nature/4312591.stm.

As I think about this, I am reminded again of how remarkable the ways of God are. God does not provide indiscriminately for our needs. God provides just what we need at the time we need it. And just as the food our bodies require to keep them healthy changes from season to season, so do our spiritual requirements. There are seasons of planting when we need rich food with lots of nutrients and fertilizer—Bible study, prayer, and teaching. And there are other seasons when we seem to grow rapidly without much in the way of care. Our ministries grow and flourish, richly blessing us and others with the abundance of the harvest. Unfortunately, we often ignore the signs that indicate the harvest is over. We try to force new life and new fruit from a ministry that is about to enter a season of winter rest.

I have been through a number of seasons like this. One of the most fruitful and fulfilling episodes of my life was the twelve years I spent as medical director onboard the Mercy Ship *Anastasis*. It is hard for me to describe the joy and satisfaction I experienced as I watched people in Africa and the Caribbean Islands transformed by cleft lip and palate and eye surgeries. Toward the end of my time on the ship, I started to feel that change was coming, but I ignored it. Not surprisingly, I became ill and spent the next few years struggling with Chronic Fatigue Syndrome, a very wintery season of enforced rest. But that too has given way to another season of planting, growth and productivity. As I have discovered the joys of liturgical living and the wonders of the garden, God has allowed me to share these gifts with others in amazing ways.

Walk Through the Garden Soup

Our favorite soup over the winter season is what I call Walk Through the Garden Soup. It is made from a basic recipe with wheat berries, dried beans, canned tomatoes, and cabbage, and whatever is still flourishing outside can be added. Here is my favorite version of this recipe:

1 cup dried beans, use scarlet runners from garden if available.
1 cup wheat berries soaked in water for 8 hours
2 tbsp olive oil
1 cup onion, chopped
4 cloves garlic, minced
1 tbsp fresh sage, chopped
1 tbsp fresh rosemary, chopped
1 lb tomatoes, chopped or 14-oz can, diced
6 cups broth, vegetable or chicken
2 lb winter squash, peeled and cut into ½-inch chunks
½ lb green beans, trimmed and cut in ½-inch lengths
1 cup carrot, peeled and cut in ½-inch chunks
1 lb cabbage, coarsely chopped
1 lb mushrooms, chopped
¼ cup parsley, chopped
1 tsp salt
Pinch of ground pepper
¾ cups Parmesan cheese, freshly grated

Soak beans and wheat berries in separate bowls overnight. Drain and set aside. Cook dried beans until just tender (45 min–1 hour). In a large pot or Dutch oven, heat oil over medium heat. Add onion and cook, stirring until soft. Add garlic, sage, and rosemary. Cook, stirring until fragrant, about 1 minute. Add wheat berries, tomatoes, broth, and water. Bring to a simmer cover and simmer until wheat ber-ries are al dente, (1–1½ hours). Add squash, green beans, carrots, cabbage, mushrooms, and reserved dried beans with their liquid. Cover and simmer until all vegetables are tender. (15–20 minutes) Stir in parsley and season with salt and pepper. Serve garnished with Parmesan cheese.

Recipes for Giving Thanks

Here are a few more of my favorite recipes for using garden produce, though I suggest that you ex-periment with your own ideas. This is a great place to use the gift of creativity that God blesses us all with.

Hunza Pie

Here is my version of the Hunza pie, which was popular among vegetarians and hippies in the 1980s. This vegetarian pie, supposedly inspired by the Hunza people of Northern Pakistan, is both nutritious and easy to make. Because it keeps well, I often make two pies at a time. It is also good for picnics and camping. I like to serve it with tomato chutney.

PASTRY	FILLING
1 1/2 cups whole wheat flour	20 stalks Swiss chard or collard greens
1 teaspoon salt	1 lb potatoes
1 1/2 cups wheat germ	1 medium onion chopped
125 gm (4 oz) margarine or butter	2 cups cottage cheese
1 egg	2 tablespoons fresh basil
2 - 3 tablespoons water (approx)	1/4 teaspoon mixed herbs
	1 teaspoon vegetable salt

Process flour, salt, wheat germ, and butter in a food processor until the mixture resembles fine bread-crumbs. Add egg and water. Process again, adding extra water if needed, to form a soft dough. Knead on a floured surface until smooth. Press into 2 x 15cm discs. Wrap in grease-proof paper. Refrigerate for 20 min. Roll out two-thirds of the pastry and place on bottom and sides of a greased 9-inch pie dish.

Wash and chop chard, removing stalks if desired. Steam or cover with small amount of water and boil until tender. Drain well. Peel potatoes, cut into cubes, and cook in salted water until tender. Drain well. Cook onion in a small amount of oil in a skillet until translucent. Combine chard, potatoes, onion, cot-tage cheese, basil, mixed herbs, and salt. Mix well. Allow to cool, then spoon over pastry. Roll out re-maining pastry, cover, brush the edges with water, and press together. Make slits in top of pastry. Brush pastry with water or egg white. Bake at 375°F for 15 minutes then reduce heat to 350°F for a fur-ther 15 to 20 minutes until golden brown. Serve hot or cold.

Green Tomato Salsa

A couple of years ago, we ended the season with 30 pounds of green toma-toes, and I had to figure out what to do with them. I experimented with all the green tomato salsa recipes I could find and came up with my own version that combined our favorite Mexican flavors together.

4 lbs green tomatoes
1 red bell pepper
1 yellow bell pepper
1 large onion, chopped
½ c. jalapeno

1 c. lemon juice
1 c. lime juice
2 tsp salt
1 Tbsp honey

Cut bell peppers in half and place under broiler until skin is blackened. Cut to-matoes in half and place under broiler until blackened Chop all ingredients and place in large pan. Boil for 20 minutes. Pack in sterilized jars.

Northwest Hot Sauce

So many hot sauce recipes use ingredients that are only available in the tropics. In this recipe, I have adapted the traditional hot sauce recipe to work with fruit and vegetables that are abundant in the Pa-cific Northwest. This makes a great accompaniment to tortilla chips.

1 lb hot peppers—cayenne, Bulgarian carrot, or jalapeno
3 c. apple cider vinegar
2 lbs tomatillos
2 lbs apple, cored and sliced
2 lbs carrot
1 onion
6 cloves garlic
½ c. lemon juice
1 tsp mustard seed
1½ tsp salt

Cut stems off peppers and put in quart jar. Fill jar with vinegar, cover and let marinate for at least 5 days to 2 weeks. When ready to prepare hot sauce, pour peppers and vinegar into blender. Add re-maining ingredients and simmer uncovered on low heat, stirring frequently for about one hour until sauce is consistency of tomato sauce. Pour into sterilized jars. Let flavors blend for at least a week be-fore using. Store in refrigerator after opening.

Roasted Tomato Marinara Sauce

This is my favorite marinara sauce, and we often make 20 to 25 quarts over the harvest season. The advantage to me is that it can be made in small quantities with the tomatoes cooking in the oven while I am busy on some writing project. The canning part is a welcome break in my day.

10 lbs tomatoes, halved
1 large onion, diced
½ c. fresh basil, chopped
6 cloves garlic, minced
1 c. red wine
1 c. water
1 tsp olive oil

Spread out tomatoes in large baking dish, sprinkle onion and garlic over top. Place in 350°F oven for 2 hours, stirring occasionally. Add water if liquid dries out. Add red wine and cook a further ½ hour. Add basil and remove from oven. Makes 4 quarts. Pour into sterilized jars and process in water bath for 30 minutes.

Frannie's Apple Cake

This recipe is adapted from one given to me by my friend, Janet Hutchison. Janet's grandmother be-came a widow with seven children, all under the age of thirteen, when she was still in her thirties. She was still climbing her apple trees to prune and spray even in her seventies. Janet was fortunate enough to grow up

6 c. apples, peeled and diced
1½ c. sugar
½ c. oil
1 c. walnuts, chopped
2 eggs, beaten
2 tsp vanilla
½ c. yogurt
1 c. all-purpose flour
1 c. whole wheat flour

2 tsp cinnamon
2 tsp baking soda
1 tsp salt

TOPPING
2 tsp cinnamon
1/3 c. brown sugar
2 tsp flour
¼ c. rolled oats

living next door and enjoyed her fresh pies, cookies, and this:

Stir together apples, sugar, oil, nuts, eggs, vanilla, and yogurt. Sift flour, cinna-mon, baking soda, and salt. Add flour mix to apple mixture. Bake in a 9"x13" pan at 350°F for about 45 min or until toothpick comes out dry. Freezes well. Serve with ice cream or whipped cream.

Top before baking with cinnamon, brown sugar, flour, and rolled oats.

If you want a more decadent cake, top with Cream cheese frosting: 8 oz cream cheese, 3 Tbsp margarine, 1 tsp vanilla, and 1½ cup powdered sugar. Makes about 15 servings.

AUTUMN: A SEASON OF OVERWHELMING ABUNDANCE 109

Praying in the Garden

Garden Blessings

God Bless This Garden

God bless this garden

Through which your glory shines

May we see in its beauty the wonder of your love.

God bless this soil

Rich and teeming with life

May we see in its fertility the promise of new creation

God bless our toil

As we dig deep to turn the soil

May we see in our labour your call to be good stewards

God bless each seed

That takes root and grows

May we see in its flourishing the hope of transformation

God bless the spring and autumn rains

That water our efforts to bring forth life

May we see in their constancy God's faithful care

God bless the harvest

Abundant and bountiful in season

May we see in God's generosity our need to share

God bless this garden

As you bless all creation with your love

May we see in its glory your awesome majesty

Amen

A Blessing for the Planting of a New Garden

God bless this soil rich and fertile with life

God bless the seed we plant this day

As it falls into the ground to grow

We remember Christ's body broken for us

Unless a seed is planted in the soil and dies

It remains alone

But its death will produce many new seeds

A plentiful harvest of new lives

In the name of God the creator,

We sprinkle it with the water of life

Remembering that though we may plant and water

It is God who give growth to all our efforts

Neither the one who plants nor the one who waters is anything,

But only God, who makes things grow.

The one who plants and the one who waters have one purpose,

and they will each be rewarded according to their own labor.

For we are God's co-workers; you are God's field, God's building .

In the name of Christ our redeemer,

We bury it deep in the ground

Waiting for the first sprout of new creation

The promise of resurrection held in each tiny kernel

Open up O heavens and pour our your righteousness

Let the earth open wide

So salvation and righteousness can sprout up together

I the Lord created them

In the name of the Spirit our counsellor,

We lay it down,

Into the cycle of living and dying and rising again

Remembering that one day all things will be made new

Look I am making all things new...

On each side of the river grew a tree of life

Bearing twelve crops of fruit with a fresh crop each month

The leaves were used for medicine to heal the nations

AMEN

Morning and Evening Prayers for Gardeners

For the last couple of years, the members of the Mustard Seed House have joined me at least once a month for a gardening day. We usually start with breakfast and then garden for a couple of hours. One of the first times we weeded together was a pretty typical autumn day in Seattle—not too cold, but rainy and definitely soggy. The rain had loosened up all the weeds and made them easy to pull. When we finished, we sat around drinking tea and coffee and eating apple cake made from the fruit of our bumper apple crop. Then we read the liturgy used here for morning prayers. My awareness of God's presence with us as we read the prayers astounded me. Gardening has always been an important part of the rhythm of my life, but this was the first time I had ever connected it in such a hands-on way to the scriptures and the wonderful sense of God's participation in creation. It made me realize how dis-connected my spiritual practices usually were from everyday life and how much more intimate my re-lationship with God can become when I connect them. I have found that reading prayers while garden-ing not only increases my enjoyment of the garden, but has also deep-ened my intimacy with God.

Morning Prayer

God of wind and storm, God of trees and flowers,
God of birds and beasts, God of men and women,
God who gave birth to all creation,
Come down this day and dwell amongst us.

Pause to reflect on the glory of God reflected in the created world.

God, your world is translucent,
Through all creation your glory shines.
God, all of life reflects your creative presence and sustaining love.
God, we see you in the wind and calm,
We see you in the sun and moon.
God, all of life reflects your creative presence and sustaining love.
God, we hear you in the song of birds and bees,
We hear you in the crash of waves and waterfalls,
God, all of life reflects your creative presence and sustaining love.
God, we feel you in warmth of sun and cold of ice,
We feel you in the richness of soil and softness of fur.
God, all of life reflects your creative presence and sustaining love.
God, we smell you in the perfume of rose and jasmine,
We smell you in the aroma of fresh cut apple and peach.
God, all of life reflects your creative presence and sustaining love.
God, we see you in the rich abundance of the harvest,
God, we hear you in the voices of those who enjoy its bounty.
God, all of life reflects your creative presence and sustaining love.
God, we feel you in the care of those with whom we share its generosity,
God, we know you in your love and care for all creation.
God, all of life reflects your creative presence and sustaining love.

Psalm 65: 5–12

You answer us with awesome and righteous deeds, God our Savior, the hope of all the ends of the earth and of the farthest seas, who formed the mountains by your power, having armed yourself with strength, who stilled the roaring of the seas, the roaring of their waves, and the turmoil of the nations.

The whole earth is filled with awe at your wonders; where morning dawns, where evening fades, you call forth songs of joy.

You care for the land and water it; you enrich it abundantly.

The streams of God are filled with water to provide the people with grain, for so you have ordained it.

You drench its furrows and level its ridges; you soften it with showers and bless its crops.

You crown the year with your bounty, and your carts overflow with abundance.

The grasslands of the wilderness overflow; the hills are clothed with gladness.

God, you call forth songs of joy from all the earth.

Ezekiel 34:25–27

"I will make a covenant of peace with them and rid the land of savage beasts so that they may live in the wilderness and sleep in the forests in safety. I will make them and the places surrounding my hill a blessing. I will send down showers in season; there will be showers of blessing. The trees will yield their fruit and the ground will yield its crops; the people will be secure in their land. They will know that I am the LORD, when I break the bars of their yoke and rescue them from the hands of those who enslaved them."

God, you call forth songs of joy from all the earth.

Colossians 1: 15–20

The Son is the image of the invisible God, the firstborn over all creation. For in him all things were created: things in heaven and on earth, visible and invisible, whether thrones or powers or rulers or authorities; all things have been created through him and for him. He is before all things, and in him all things hold together. And he is the head of the body, the church; he is the beginning and the firstborn from among the dead, so that in everything he might have the supremacy. For God was pleased to have all his fullness dwell in him, and through him to reconcile to himself all things, whether things on earth or things in heaven, by making peace through his blood, shed on the cross.

God, you call forth songs of joy from all the earth.

Matthew 6: 25–33

"Therefore I tell you, do not worry about your life, what you will eat or drink; or about your body, what you will wear. Is not life more important than food, and the body more important than clothes? Look at the birds of the air; they do not sow or reap or store away in barns, and yet your heavenly Father feeds them. Are you not much more valuable than they? Can any one of you by worrying add a single hour to your life?

"And why do you worry about clothes? See how the flowers of the field grow. They do not labor or spin. Yet I tell you that not even Solomon in all his splendor was dressed like one of these. If that is how God clothes the grass of the field, which is here today and tomorrow is thrown into the fire, will he not much more clothe you—you of little faith? So do not worry, saying, 'What shall we eat?' or 'What shall we drink?' or 'What shall we wear?' For the pagans run after all these things, and your heavenly Father knows that you need them. But seek first his kingdom and his righteousness, and all these things will be given to you as well."

God, you call forth songs of joy from all the earth.

We believe in God above us,

Creator of all things, sustainer of all life.

We believe in Christ beside us,

Companion and friend, redeemer of all the broken pieces of our universe.

We believe in Spirit deep within us,

Advocate and guide, who lives with us eternally.

We believe in God's resurrection created world,

Where all things are fixed, and all creation fits together in vibrant harmonies.

We believe in God above, beside, within,

God yesterday, today and forever, the three in one, the one in three,

We believe in God.

Our Father in heaven, hallowed be your name. Your Kingdom come, your will be done, on earth as in heaven. Give us today our daily bread. Forgive us our sins, as we forgive those who sin against us. Lead us not into temptation, but deliver us from evil. For the kingdom, the power and the glory are yours. Now and forever. Amen.

Upon all farmers, market gardeners, foresters and all who work the land,

Lord, have mercy

Upon ranchers, zoo keepers, veterinarians and all who work with animals

Lord, have mercy

Upon all fisherman, sailors and those who work on the sea

Lord, have mercy

Upon all whose homes are destroyed by tsunami or earthquake or hurricane

Christ, have mercy

Upon all whose land has been spoiled by drought or flood or war

Christ, have mercy

Upon all those who suffer through pollution and destruction of creation,

Christ, have mercy

Upon conservationists, park rangers, and all who care for God's good creation,

Lord, have mercy

Upon landscape gardeners, horticulturalists and all who preserve and restore the earth's beauty

Lord, have mercy

Upon all God's creatures, great and small, and on all who care for their environment

Lord, have mercy

God almighty, creator of all life, the One who fixes all the broken places of our universe, the work of your hands reflects your great love and concern for all creation. May we be wise stewards and ensure that nothing you have made is spoiled or misused. May we share generously and justly from your rich and abundant resources. Jesus Christ, who gave yourself for our world, unite us through your cove-nant of peace, so that all peoples of the earth may share your lavish bounty together.

Life of God be with you this day,
Love of the Creator fill your heart,
Light of the Savior guide your steps,
Hope of the Sanctifier teach your minds,
Life of the Three sustain you,
Love of the One encircle you,
Now and always, this day and forever,
Amen

Evening Prayer

God who makes the crops to grow,

God who feeds the birds and beasts,

Refresh us this night and protect us from harm.

God who heals our wounds and pain,

God who brings us peace and rest,

Refresh us this night and protect us from harm.

Pause to reflect on what you have learned through God's created world today.

For the music of our world,

The divine song that sings through all creation,

God our creator, we praise you.

For the beauty of all you have created,

A mirror of the wonders of heaven,

God our creator, we praise you.

For the resounding roar of thunder,

Your awesome majesty revealed,

God our creator, we praise you.

For a clouded sky splashed with sunset colors,

A glimpse of heaven's glory,

God our creator, we praise you.

For the fragrance of a rose,

Your sweet perfume of grace,

God our creator, we praise you.

For a riotous field of wildflowers,

God's exuberant laughter unfolded,

God our creator, we praise you.

For a snowflake, an atom, a mathematical formula,

A hint of your unimagined complexity,

God our creator, we praise you.

For the call to steward your creation,

To tend your garden and make it flourish,

God our creator, we praise you.

Psalm 148

Praise the LORD.

Praise the LORD from the heavens; praise him in the heights above.

Praise him, all his angels; praise him, all his heavenly hosts.

Praise him, sun and moon; praise him, all you shining stars.

Praise him, you highest heavens and you waters above the skies.

Let them praise the name of the LORD, for at his command they were created, and he established them for ever and ever—he issued a decree that will never pass away.

Praise the LORD from the earth, you great sea creatures and all ocean depths, lightning and hail, snow and clouds, stormy winds that do his bidding, you mountains and all hills, fruit trees and all cedars, wild animals and all cattle, small creatures and flying birds, kings of the earth and all nations, you princes and all rulers on earth, young men and women, old men and children.

Let them praise the name of the LORD, for his name alone is exalted; his splendor is above the earth and the heavens. And he has raised up for his people a horn, the praise of all his faithful servants, of Israel, the people close to his heart.

Praise the LORD.

Isaiah 35:1–7

The desert and the parched land will be glad; the wilderness will rejoice and blossom. Like the crocus, it will burst into bloom; it will rejoice greatly and shout for joy. The glory of Lebanon will be given to it, the splendor of Carmel and Sharon; they will see the glory of the LORD, the splendor of our God.

Strengthen the feeble hands, steady the knees that give way; say to those with fearful hearts, "Be strong, do not fear; your God will come, he will come with vengeance; with divine retribution he will come to save you."

Then will the eyes of the blind be opened and the ears of the deaf unstopped Then will the lame leap like a deer, and the mute tongue shout for joy. Water will gush forth in the wilderness and streams in the desert. The burning sand will become a pool, the thirsty ground bubbling springs. In the haunts where jackals once lay, grass and reeds and papyrus will grow.

Romans 8:19–21

The creation waits in eager expectation for the children of God to be revealed. For the creation was subjected to frustration, not by its own choice, but by the will of the one who subjected it, in hope that the creation itself will be liberated from its bondage to decay and brought into the freedom and glory of the children of God.

John 15:1–8

"I am the true vine, and my Father is the gardener. He cuts off every branch in me that bears no fruit, while every branch that does bear fruit he prunes so that it will be even more fruitful. You are already clean because of the word I have spoken to you. Remain in me, as I also remain in you. No branch can bear fruit by itself; it must remain in the vine. Neither can you bear fruit unless you remain in me.

"I am the vine; you are the branches. If you remain in me and I in you, you will bear much fruit; apart from me you can do nothing. If you do not remain in me, you are like a branch that is thrown away and withers; such branches are picked up, thrown into the fire and burned. If you remain in me and my words remain in you, ask whatever you wish, and it will be done for you. This is to my Father's glory, that you bear much fruit, showing yourselves to be my disciples.

God, we believe all creation waits in anticipation for Christ's return,

When your creative power will transform all of life,

And you will give birth to a resurrection world of fairness and freedom.

The difficult times of pain will be turned into songs of joy.

Scarcity will be transformed into abundance.

Greed will be replaced by generosity.

Oppression will be overcome by justice.

God, we believe that when your new world of wholeness and shalom is born,

Your healing power will be unleashed in its fullness:

The blind will see and the lame leap like deer,

Righteousness and faithfulness will reign,

The voiceless will break into song, and streams will flow in the desert.

All of creation will find its true purpose in Christ.

Our Father in heaven, hallowed be your name. Your Kingdom come, your will be done, on earth as in heaven. Give us today our daily bread. Forgive us our sins, as we forgive those who sin against us. Lead us not into temptation, but deliver us from evil. For the kingdom, the power and the glory are yours. Now and forever. Amen.

Faithful God, creator of all times and seasons,
We so easily forget that hidden within the night's dark embrace are the seeds
    of life.
Remind us, loving God, that when all seems dark and empty,
You are still at work strengthening our roots, healing our wounds, anchoring
    our lives.
Remind us, generous God, that when morning dawns,
It is the night's long rest that has sustained and nurtured our souls.
Keep us, faithful God, through the dark journey of life,
So that when the new dawn breaks our roots may be deep and strong.

Deep peace of the running wave to you,
Deep peace of the flowing air to you,
Deep peace of the quiet earth to you,
Deep peace of the shining stars to you,
Deep peace of the Son of peace to you forever.

Deep peace of the God of life to you,
Deep peace of the Christ of love to you,
Deep peace of the Spirit of truth to you,
Deep peace of the God of Gods to you,
The peace of all peace be yours this night and forevermore,

Amen

Resources

Books

Organic Gardening Essentials

1. Mel Bartholomew, *Square Foot Gardening* (Emmaus, Penn.: Rodale Press, 1981).

2. Wendell Berry, *Life Is A Mystery: An Essay Against Modern Superstition* (Counterpoint, 2001).

3. Eliot Coleman, *The New Organic Grower: A Master's Manuel of Tools and Techniques for the Home and Market Gardener* (White River Junction, Ver.: Chelsea Green Publishing, 1995).

4. Joan Dye Gussow, *This Organic Life: Confessions of a Suburban Homesteader* (White River Junction, Ver.: Chelsea Green Publishing, 2001).

5. Sharon Lovejoy, *A Blessing of Toads: A Gardener's Guide to Living With Nature* (New York: Hearst Books, 2004).

6. Michael Pollan, *Second Nature: A Gardener's Education* (Grove Press, 1991).

7. Steve Solomon, *Growing Vegetables West of the Cascades: Steve Solomon's Complete Guide to Natural Gardening* (Seattle, Wash.: Sasquatch Books, 1989).

8. *The Maritime Northwest Garden Guide* (Seattle Tilth Association, 2000).

Spirituality of Gardening

1. Brother Victor-Antoine d'Avila-Latourrette, *A Monastic Year: Reflections From a Monastery* (Dallas, Tex.: Taylor Publishing, 1996).

2. Maureen Gilmer, *Rooted in the Spirit: Exploring Inspirational Gardens* (Dallas, Tex.: Taylor Publishing, 1997).

3. Vigen Guroian, *Inheriting Paradise: Meditations on Gardening* (Grand Rapids, Mich.: Eerdmans Publishing, 1999).

4. Wendy Johnson, *Gardening at the Dragon's Gate: At Work in the Wild and Cultivated World* (New York: Bantam Books, 2008).

5. Esther De Waal, *The Celtic Way of Prayer: The Recovery of the Religious Imagination* (New York: Doubleday, 1997).

Websites

Garden Seed and Supplies

1. Bountiful Gardens, www.bountifulgardens.org
2. Gardener's Supply, www.gardenersupply.com
3. Peaceful Valley Farm & Garden Supply, www.groworganic.com
4. Park's Seed, www.parkseed.com/gardening
5. Seed Savers Exchange, www.seedsavers.org
6. Seeds of Change, www.seedsofchange.com
7. Territorial Seeds, www.territorialseed.com
8. Totally Tomatoes, www.totallytomato.com
9. Thompson & Morgan Seeds, www.tmseeds.com
10. Vesey's Seeds, www.veseys.com
11. Victory Seeds, www.victoryseeds.com
12. West Coast Seeds, www.westcoastseeds.com

Garden Advice and Planning

1. BBC's virtual garden planner, www.bbc.co.uk/gardening/design
2. Dirt Doctor, www.dirtdoctor.com
3. Edible Seattle, www.ediblecommunities.com/seattle
4. Gardens Alive, www.gardensalive.com
5. Plan Garden, www.plangarden.com
6. Organic Gardening, www.organicgardening.com
7. Urban Garden Share, Seattle Wash., www.urbangardenshare.org
8. Canadian Wildlife Federation, www.wildaboutgardening.org
9. Gardener's Supply Kitchen Garden Planning, http://www.gardeners.com/on/demandware.store/Sites-Gardeners-Site/default/Page-KitchenGardenDesigner

Sustainable Living and Creation Care

1. A Rocha: Christians in Creation Care, www.arocha.org
2. Christian Simple Living, www.christiansimpleliving.com
3. Earth Ministry, www.earthministry.org
4. European Christian Environmental Network, www.ecen.org
5. Evangelical Environmental Network, www.creationcare.org
6. Flourish: a collaborative environmental network, www.flourishonline.org
7. Sustainable Traditions, www.sustainabletraditions.com

Creating a Faith-Based Community Garden

1. Montgomery Victory Gardens: Tips For Starting a Faith Based Community Garden, http://www.montgomeryvictorygardens.org/documents/pdf/Tips for FBCG.pdf
2. The Brown Bag Series sponsored by the Community Partnership Project at the University of Missouri, http://umslce.org/index.php/centers-a-programs/community-partnership-project
3. St. Louis: Faith Based and Neighbourhood Partnerships in the Age of Obama, http://umslce.org/index.php/brown-bag-series
4. North Carolina State University Community Gardens: Eat Smart, Move More North Carolina: Growing Communities Through Gardens, http://nccommunitygarden.ncsu.edu/primer.html
5. Seattle Public Utilities Natural Lawn and Garden Care provides a variety of downloadable resources, http://www.seattle.gov/util/Services/Yard/Natural_Lawn_&_Garden_Care/index.asp :

Blogs on Faith-Based Gardening

1. Sparks in the Soil, soilsparks.typepad.com
2. The Pumpkin Patch Community Garden, www.millwoodpc.org/Mission/PumpkinPatchCommunityGarden
3. Five Loaves Farm, fiveloavesfarm.blogspot.com
4. Sustainable Northwest: Interfaith Network for Earth Concerns, www.sustainablenorthwest.org/stories/interfaith-network-for-earth-concerns

The Monthly Garden Planting and Harvest Guide

The following chart is a record of my own personal activities in the garden. It is fairly specifically geared towards the Seattle area, but you can adjust it quite simply if you know the frost dates—the average date of the last frost in the spring and the first frost in the autumn. There are numerous websites where you can find these, though I must confess that they all seem to list different dates. The most comprehensive site I have found, which has first and last frost dates not just for the US, but also for Canada, Europe, Australia, and China, is Victory Seeds (www.victoryseeds.com).

Seattle's average last frost date is estimated between mid-March and mid-April probably because micro-climates play an important role in frost dates. Hills and water can significantly affect temperatures and so a neighbor's yard on a small hill or in a valley may have a different date from yours. So this is really something that you learn over many years of experience.

I suggest that gardeners keep their own garden journal and harvest record. I find that this helps tremendously for planning the next year. I know I can't always remember when I need to plant and transplant my seeds in order to produce the optimal harvest. I also love to take photos, and this can provide an even better record of what goes on in both your vegetable and flower gardens.

Seattle Summary

January	12 weeks before last frost
February	8 weeks before last frost
March	4 weeks before last frost
mid-April	safe last frost date
mid-May	safe for planting warm-weather crops
June & July	plant crops for autumn harvest
mid-October	last harvest before frost
mid-November	average first frost

Symbols Key

 Plant Indoors

 Plant / Transplant Outdoors

 Harvest

RESOURCES 135

	Artichokes	Beans, Scarlet	Beans, Bush	Beans, Fava	Beets	Broccoli, Green	Broccoli, Overwinter	Brussel Sprouts	Cabbage, Red Spring
January									
February						🜉	🕷		🜉
March							🕷		
April						🐞	🜉		🜉
May		🐞	🐞	🕷		🕷			🕷
June					🐞	🜉	🜉	🜉	🜉
July					🐞		🐞		
August		🕷	🕷		🕷				🕷
September		🕷	🕷	🐞	🕷	🕷			
October		🕷			🕷	🕷			
November					🕷	🕷			🕷
December								🕷	🕷

	Cabbage, Savoy	Carrots, Summer	Carrots, Overwinter	Cauliflower, Ravella	Cauliflower, Spring	Cucumber	Eggplant	Garlic	Greens, Bok Choy
January		🕷	🕷						
February		🕷	🕷		🪰				🪰
March		🐞	🕷		🪰		🪰		🐞
April		🐞			🐞	🪰			
May		🐞			🕷	🐞	🐞		🕷
June	🪰	🐞		🪰	🕷	🐞		🕷	🕷
July	🐞	🐞		🐞		🕷	🕷	🕷	
August		🕷				🕷	🕷	🕷	
September		🕷	🐞				🕷		🐞
October		🕷		🕷				🐞	
November	🕷	🕷		🕷					🕷
December	🕷	🕷							🕷

RESOURCES 137

	Greens, Chard	Greens, Kale	Greens, Kizuna	Greens, Mizpoona	Greens, Spinach	Greens, Tat-soi	Herbs, Basil	Herbs, Dill	Herbs, Parsley
January		🕷	🕷	🕷					
February		🕷	🪰		🪰	🪰			
March	🪰		🐞	🐞	🐞	🐞			
April	🐞		🕷	🐞	🕷	🕷		🪰	🐞
May		🪰	🕷	🕷		🐞		🐞	
June	🪰	🐞	🕷	🕷		🐞	🕷		🕷
July	🐞	🐞		🕷		🕷	🕷		🕷
August			🐞		🐞	🐞	🕷	🕷	🕷
September	🕷		🐞	🐞	🐞	🐞	🕷	🕷	🕷
October	🕷	🕷				🕷	🕷	🕷	🕷
November	🕷	🕷	🕷	🕷	🕷	🕷		🕷	
December		🕷	🕷	🕷	🕷			🕷	

	Leeks, Overwinter	Leeks, Varna	Lettuce, Spring	Lettuce, Summer	Lettuce, Fall	Lettuce, Winter	Lettuce, Overwinter	Onions, Red	Onions, Walla Walla
January	🕷	🪰					🕷	🪰	
February	🕷		🪰				🕷	🐞	🐞
March	🪰		🐞						
April			🕷	🐞					
May			🕷	🐞					
June			🕷	🕷	🐞			🕷	🕷
July				🕷	🐞			🕷	🕷
August				🕷		🐞			
September					🕷	🐞	🐞		
October		🕷			🕷				
November	🕷	🕷			🕷	🕷			
December	🕷	🕷				🕷			

	Onions, Green	Peas	Potatoes	Peppers, Mild	Peppers, Hot	Squash, Summer	Squash, Winter	Tomatoes	Tomatillos
January	🪰	🪰							
February		🐞	🐞						
March	🕷			🪰	🪰	🪰	🪰	🪰	🪰
April	🐞								
May	🕷	🕷		🐞	🐞	🐞	🐞	🐞	🐞
June	🐞	🕷							
July	🕷							🕷	🕷
August	🕷		🕷	🕷		🕷		🕷	🕷
September	🕷	🐞	🕷	🕷	🕷	🕷		🕷	🕷
October		🐞			🕷	🕷	🕷	🕷	🕷
November							🕷		
December									

Harvest Log

CROP	Date/Weight	Date/Weight	Date/Weight	Date/Weight

Date/Weight	Date/Weight	Date/Weight	Date/Weight	Date/Weight	Date/Weight	Date/Weight

CROP	Date/Weight	Date/Weight	Date/Weight	Date/Weight

Date/ Weight	Date/ Weight	Date/ Weight	Date/ Weight	Date/ Weight	Date/ Weight	Date/ Weight

 **Christine Sine** is the Executive Director of Mustard Seed Associates (www.msainfo.org). She trained as a physician in Australia and developed the medical ministry for Mercy Ships. She now lives in Seattle with her husband Tom Sine as part of the Mustard Seed House community (mustardseedhouse.wordpress.com). She is an avid gardener with a growing passion to enable followers of Christ to connect their faith to everyday life. She speaks on issues relating to how to change our timestyle and lifestyle to develop a more spiritual rhythm for life that interweaves throughout every aspect of life. She has authored several books including Godspace and Living on Purpose. She blogs at godspace.wordpress.com.

Mustard Seed Associates is a small non-profit organization that raises awareness of challenges Christians will face in life, church and community in the future. We seek to foster spirituality that draws followers of Christ into a deeper relationship with God and encourage innovation that enables us to create new ways to advance God's kingdom purposes and engage tomorrow's challenges. MSA is also a crossroads, grassroots organization—connecting people across generations, denominations and cultures and equipping them to creatively transform their cultures by both living differently and making a difference for God's kingdom. For more information visit our website at www.msainfo.org.

To Garden With God
A Seminar with Christine Sine

Do you struggle to connect to the story of God through morning devotions and Sunday worship? I believe one reason people are moving away from Christianity at time-warp speed is because we have divorced our faith from the glory of God revealed through the natural world. Nothing makes me more aware of this than working in the garden. I read about the death and resurrection of Christ in the Bible, but I experience it every time I plant a seed and watch it burst into life. I read about the faithfulness of God to Israel but I experience it every time I watch the rain fall and nourish the seeds I have planted. I read about the miracle of the fish and the loaves but I experience a miracle every time I am overwhelmed by the generosity of God's harvest.

In this workshop, we will discuss the wonderful ways that God is revealed through the rhythms of planting, growing, and harvesting in the garden. There will be spiritual insights and practical suggestions for backyard gardening in the Northwest. Come prepared to get your hands (and your clothes) dirty!

This seminar is based on the the reflections in *To Garden with God*. Christine hosts one or two seminars at the Mustard Seed House in the spring. If you are interested in a seminar in your area, please contact her at seasickdoctor@gmail.com.

Other MSA Resources

E-books and Media

To Garden With God
by **Christine Sine**

A manual for backyard organic gardening prepared by Christine Sine for spring workshops. This resource mixes practical advice with spiritual reflections on creation and God's great bounty.

Turbulent Times—Ready or Not!
by **Tom Sine**

In these changing economic times, how can churches and individuals better respond to the needs of vulnerable neighbors and be good stewards of their resources?

Justice at the Table
by **Ricci Kilmer**

This resource is a collection of personal reflections and practical ideas to help us redeem "food" in all its dimensions—from its mundane place as an annoying chore to a spiritual practice essential to a life of faith. Take a look and see how you can continue to redeem your relationship with food for the kingdom of God.

A Journey Into Wholeness: Lenten Reflection Guide
by **Christine Sine**

A five-week study with reflections, litanies, and activities exploring our brokenness and the suffering of Jesus Christ as he journeyed toward the cross.

A Journey Into God's Resurrection-Created World: An Easter Celebration Guide
by **Christine Sine**

In these changing economic times, how can churches and individuals better respond to the needs of vulnerable neighbors and be good stewards of their resources?

Advent Reflection Videos
by Christine Sine

Every year, Christine creates another meditation on the coming of Christ. Titles include "The Coming of the Lord Is Near," "Waiting for the Light," and "Awaiting the Christ Child." Available at stores.lulu.com/mail1058

Recordings from Past Events

Did you miss our conferences the past few years? For just a couple bucks you can hear from Shane Claiborne, Efrem Smith, Lisa Domke, Mark Scandrette, Eliacin Rosario-Cruz, just to name a few. Available at stores.lulu.com/mail1058

Books by MSA Staff
Available at www.msainfo.org/store

Godspace: Time for Peace in the Rhythms of Life
by Christine Sine (Barclay Books, 2006)

Living On Purpose: Finding God's Best for Your Life
by Christine and Tom Sine (Baker Books, 2002)

Travel Well: Maintaining Physical, Spiritual, and Emotional Health During International Ministry
by Christine Aroney-Sine, M.D. (World Vision, 2005)

Tales of a Seasick Doctor: Life Aboard a Mercy Ship
by Christine Aroney-Sine, M.D. (Zondervan, 1996)

The New Conspirators: Creating the Future One Mustard Seed at a Time
by Tom Sine (InterVarsity Press, 2008)

Mustard Seed vs McWorld: Reinventing Life and Faith for the Future
by Tom Sine (Baker Books, 1999)

Made in the USA
Charleston, SC
17 February 2012